"Matt Woodley points the way by reminding us of a tradition that is firmly rooted in Scripture and the life of Christ, but which has been largely lost. If we love God enough to love his world, we would do well to reflect on whether the holy fools of history can teach us something significant about faithfully engaging our world with the gospel."

DENIS D. HAACK
Founder, Ransom Fellowship

"Some books on 'spirituality' are so narcissistic they give me hives. But this is the real deal: It's ancient and fresh, self-deprecating and reader-challenging, irritating and soothing. Matt Woodley is a funny guy. He's also a gifted writer, a gentle pastor, an insightful guide. His book challenged me and made me want to grow up."

KEVIN MILLER
Executive Vice President, Christianity Today International

"With humility and an unhindered transparency, Mathew Woodley writes this refreshing wake-up call to those of us bored with today's deeply rutted, trudging Christian journey. A must-read for those who dare to leave footprints today."

REV. BILL SENYARD
New Life Church at Five Points, Montgomeryville, Pennsylvania

"This book serves up a literary feast usually found only in secular writers and laureates. Those wild and wooly desert fathers have never been in better hands than Woodley's."

LEONARD SWEET
Professor, Drew Theological School and George Fox University

"Passionately, thoughtfully, and humorously, Mathew Woodley introduces us to his most unlikely band of spiritual mentors and their Christlike approach to the spiritual life."

MICHAEL GLERUP
Project director, Center for Early African Christianity

HOLY FOOLS

Following Jesus with Reckless Abandon

MATHEW WOODLEY

SALT**RIVER**®

AN IMPRINT OF

TYNDALE HOUSE PUBLISHERS, INC.
CAROL STREAM, ILLINOIS

Visit Tyndale's exciting Web site at www.tyndale.com

Holy Fools: Following Jesus with Reckless Abandon

This book is published in association with the literary agency of Sanford Communications, Inc., Portland, Oregon.

Library of Congress Cataloging-in-Publication Data

Woodley, Mathew.
   Holy fools : following Jesus with reckless abandon / Mathew Woodley.
      p. cm.
   Includes bibliographical references.
   ISBN-13: 978-1-4143-1630-7 (hc)
   ISBN-10: 1-4143-1630-5 (hc)
1. Holy fools.   2. Christian life.   I. Title.
BX323.W66 2008
248.4—dc22   2007051551

Printed in the United States of America

14   13   12   11   10   09   08
 7   6   5   4   3   2   1

Author's Note: In order to protect privacy and confidentiality, some of the names and details in the stories have been altered.

Contents

*I happily dedicate this book to my wife, Julie. More than anyone
I know, by loving Jesus with reckless abandon, you exude—no, you ooze—
the precious and rare oil of holy folly.
I love you.*

. . .

*Thanks to David Sanford at Sanford Communications Inc. for believing
in this book when I had placed it on the shelf. To Jan Harris at Tyndale
for tweaking this book a few degrees in the right direction and breathing
new life into it. To Stephanie Voiland at Tyndale for her eye for detail and
for her vision and enthusiasm for holy folly. And to the people at Three
Village Church for loving me and my family over the past seven years.
Thank you for allowing me to "grow up" in Jesus with you.*

Holy Fools:
The Ants in Our Spiritual Pants

Only a fool would attempt to change the world with a simple
message of love and peace. So we can conclude that Jesus
was a fool. Only fools would agree to follow such a man.
. . . So we can conclude that all of us are fools. . . . So let all
happily admit that we are fools. Then we will happily commit
ourselves to change the world.

SAINT JOHN CHRYSOSTOM
(fourth century AD)

I'LL NEVER FORGET THE DAY when my friend Alan, a contemporary
holy fool, awakened my heart to love God on a deeper level.
Alan, a plump little man in his late thirties, was born with Down
syndrome. But that never stopped him from worshiping with us.
Every Sunday, Alan, our most devoted worshiper, sat in the front
pew, singing loudly and off-key and depositing a one-dollar bill
in the offering plate. More than anyone else I know, Alan is crazy
about God.

Every year Alan watched our church go through the motions
of handing out Bibles to the sixth-grade Sunday school classes.
We marched the children through the routine procedure, most of
them receiving the Bibles with blank and listless faces. Alan, the
founding member of the "Happy Friends" Sunday school class
for those with disabilities, felt a little cheated. "Hey, how come
we don't get Bibles?" he asked his teachers. Alan insisted that we
give Bibles to the Happy Friends, too.

So three months later, during our main Sunday morning worship service, Alan and the Happy Friends received their Bibles—but it was far from routine. As I gave a Bible to Alan, he started weeping. And then with dramatic flair, Alan held the Bible high over his head for thirty seconds. Everyone watched in rapt attention as he lowered the Bible to his lips, fervently kissing it and then embracing it as if it were a teddy bear. Alan continued beaming and praising God until I finally invited him to sit down.

Alan's playful, love-ravished "sermon" unsettled God's settled people. He disrupted my agenda and pierced my heart. On that Sunday morning, Alan's enthusiasm subverted our expectations, undercutting our spiritual complacency and our listless routine of worship. In the process, he awakened our hearts to the wonder of God's grace.

Such is the power of the holy fool.

Most of us are familiar with the unholy fool mentioned in Proverbs. He's the dolt who spurns advice, acts compulsively, returns to his own vomit, and chatters like a nitwit. We're told to watch this fool and then do the opposite. But most of us haven't considered the other fool mentioned in Scripture—the "holy fool," or the "fool for Christ's sake." To be honest, that phrase still grates on me. A fool for Christ? I'll gladly be "mature in Christ" or "respectable for Christ" or "Spirit-filled for Christ" or "cutting-edge for Christ." But a fool for Christ? How does that fit into a culture (and a church culture) obsessed with pragmatism, efficiency, relevance, and respectability?

And yet, we can't deny that there is a stream of holy folly running right through the Old Testament prophets, the letters from the apostle Paul (who coined the phrase "fools for Christ" [1 Corinthians 4:10]), and two thousand years of Christian spirituality. We find this stream running through the early monastic movement in "fools" known as the desert fathers and mothers—a motley bunch of fourth-century Christians who left the security of a safe but complacent, compromised church to seek God in the margins of society.[1] We also see the stream of holy folly meandering through later Christ followers such as Saint Francis of Assisi and Hudson Taylor, the forerunner of missions to China. Most important, in the life and teachings and death of Jesus, we find the ultimate expression of holy folly.

I have to warn you, though: The holy fools are a strange breed, and the stream of holy folly flows with quirky twists and turns. And yet this odd group of Jesus followers has certainly grown on me. Like a very strong espresso or a bucket of icy water dumped on my head, they provide the jolt my soul needs. When I feel lulled into spiritual slumber, they are the Spirit-inspired alarm that startles me and wakes me up. Maybe we all need a holy-fool-inspired awakening.

The holy fools often jar our sensibilities of respectable Christianity—but that is precisely the point. They don't just "fire us up." They trip us and knock us off balance. I believe the Christian community, especially in the affluent West, needs to walk with this motley band of holy fools. The stories of holy fools have provoked, stirred, disrupted, and challenged me. I hope that the stories will startle and shock us. I also hope they'll make us laugh, because the holy fools certainly have a sense of humor. More than anything, I hope they rattle our spiritual complacency, causing us to take ourselves less seriously and to take God far more seriously. To paraphrase Frederick Buechner, I hope they'll serve as the ants in the pants of our faith, crawling up our legs, getting in our underwear, itching and irritating us just enough so we can't sit still.

However, right from the start I need to issue two warning statements. *First, holy folly is not an excuse for blatant anti-intellectualism.* I meet far too many Christ followers who think authentic spirituality and stupidity (or at least anti-intellectualism) go hand in hand. I strongly disagree. Our minds are amazing instruments; God wants us to use them. Pure faith and clear thinking belong together. In this regard, I love the challenge from the brilliant scientist-theologian Dr. John Polkinghorne:

> Many people seem to think that faith involves shutting one's eyes, gritting one's teeth, and believing six impossible things before breakfast because the Bible or the Pope or some other questionable authority tells us so. Not at all! Faith may involve a leap, but it's a leap into the light, not into the dark. The aim of the religious quest, like that of the scientific quest, is to seek motivated belief about what is the case. . . . [Christianity] can only be of real value if it's actually true. It's not a technique for whistling in the dark to keep our spirits up.[2]

The holy fools often used nontraditional teaching techniques. Sometimes they eschewed logical arguments or even words. They aimed to reform our hearts and our behavior, not just give another stale lecture so we could store more information in our frontal lobes. I often say that if I consistently obeyed 3 percent of what I know about the Bible, I'd be on my way to sainthood. The holy fools assumed that most of us already have plenty of correct doctrine and biblical knowledge; they were annoyed with our lack of application. So they devised "nonrational" approaches to awaken us to specific biblical truths. And by the way, many of these nonrational approaches were brilliant in their intellectual depth and psychological effectiveness. But despite these unconventional approaches, the holy fools wouldn't tell us to bury our brains in the sand.

Second, holy folly does not demand slavish imitation. I'm a middle-aged pastor living on Long Island. I have a wife and four children, and I try to obey the law. If I walked around like the prophet Isaiah with my buttocks bared (see Isaiah 20:2), I'd probably end up in jail. My elder board loves me in all my sin and brokenness (way beyond what I deserve), but they would definitely draw the line at public nakedness, even if I was demonstrating a spiritual truth. They haven't written it into our church constitution or my employment contract, but I just have a hunch they wouldn't tolerate bare buttocks for Jesus' sake.

In other words, I cannot slavishly imitate every detail from the actions of the holy fools. I cannot wipe the snot from lepers' noses here in New York (I've never met a real leper) or move to the desert for thirty years (the nearest desert is 1,500 miles away) or throw nuts at church ladies (see chapter 1 for other such examples of holy folly). People wouldn't get the point. I can't seek to imitate all the specific actions of past holy fools; however, I do want to capture and emulate the spirit of the holy fools. I want and desperately need their immoderate passion for God. I want and desperately need their compassion for marginal people. I need their fiery quest to please God above anything else.

So before we read about and apply this holy fools stream of Christian spirituality, we'll need to refine our skills of thinking and discernment. We'll need to ponder some challenging questions: What do the holy fools mean for us today? How can we apply their extraordinary—and sometimes downright strange—behavior to our lives in this culture? And how does a middle-class, middle-aged American who may never see a real desert apply their message? Of course, I ask these questions firmly believing that, although their tactics are unusual (that's putting it mildly), they still challenge us today.

So are you ready to trade in a "nice" but bland version of Christianity for the dangerous but rewarding path of the holy fools? Are you willing to open your soul to the road that the holy fools—ancient and contemporary—have walked before us? Are you willing to be rattled out of complacency into an immoderate love for God and others? If you are willing to have your life shaken up and turned upside down for the sake of Christ, you are ready to begin the journey of holy folly.

CHAPTER 1

Discovering God's Ragged Children

There are two kinds of fools in this world: damned fools and what Saint Paul calls "fools for Christ's sake."

FREDERICK BUECHNER

ABOUT TEN YEARS AGO I served as the pastor of a thriving church in a small town in northeastern Minnesota. Everyone in the church and even the whole town liked me. I suppose it was a tiny town—about four hundred people and nine hundred dairy cows—but most of them (the people, that is) *really* liked me. They liked my sermons, my dedication, my niceness, my spiritual maturity, and my professional competence. So based on the assessment of that teeny church in that tiny town of four hundred people, I decided to like myself.

Everyone seemed to like the deal . . . except for some of my closest friends. For some reason, they thought my spiritual life was veering off course. I couldn't understand why. After all, everything seemed headed in the right direction. But as I look back on my life, I realize that they were trying to get my attention. For instance, my wife tried to tell me that in my pursuit of success I had ditched her heart. I didn't listen because I thought she was the one in need of a major spiritual awakening; I wasn't. Personally, I swallowed the press clippings about my life: "Matt is a great guy who meets our needs. Hurrah for Matt!"

Then somewhere on my path it hit me: My heart really is dead inside. Actually, it happened while I was leading a ten-day youth mission trip, crammed into large vans, sleeping in muggy church basements, and tearing off dilapidated roofs with a dozen unmotivated teenagers. This trip was one of my more "spiritual" and "sacrificial" ministry moments, but even so, deep down, I knew that my spiritual life needed a jolt, a revamping, a kick in the pants, and a major awakening. My faith had become mild, respectable, safe, reasonable, and utterly dull. I went through all the right motions and applied the right formulas, but my faith had grown complacent.

That night, alone and desperate, I hunched over the steering wheel in our church van and wept. But in that moment of desperation, God initiated a new phase in my spiritual journey. Over the next ten years God started to awaken my heart with the stunning, tangy, mysterious, delightful, surprising, and heart-ravishing good news of the Gospel. Obviously, the Holy Spirit orchestrated the entire process. Obviously, God brought me back to his Word again and again.

But along the path of this major reawakening, God also brought some powerful and wise spiritual mentors into my life. Just to warn you, this isn't exactly a touching *Tuesdays with Morrie* kind of tale. The mentors God placed in my life were, shall we say, unique. Okay, at times they were utterly bizarre. First of all, most of them have been dead for a long time. And they probably wouldn't qualify as cool and competent spiritual guides in most of our churches. As a matter of fact, most of them wouldn't qualify to write Christian books, lead church growth seminars, serve as pastors, or even pour the orange juice during our Sunday morning "bagel time." These mentors have far too many sharp, quirky, ragged edges. In the history of Christian spirituality, they're called the "Holy Fools," a strange breed of Christ followers marked by an unconventional, edgy, countercultural but entirely Christ-haunted, God-passionate, and Spirit-drunk approach to a journey with Christ. Through these unlikely guides, God gave me the jolt, the wake-up call, and the kick in the pants that I so desperately needed.

This is the story of my long, slow awakening and the strange band of ragged mentors—the holy fools—God used to lead me deeper into his grace.

Who Are the Holy Fools?

Like children playing peekaboo, the faces of God's holy fools began to jump out at me during this slow journey of reawakening to Christ. As I read the story of Christian spirituality across the ages, I noticed the startling presence of these unsettling saints who followed the path of holy folly. Let me share a few of the stories of holy fools that I encountered.

In the Old Testament I discovered a ragged gang called the prophets. "The prophets are crazy and the inspired men are fools!" according to the people in Hosea's time (see chapter 9:7). Hosea blamed the prophets' low approval rating on the hard-heartedness of the people, but one could also argue that the prophets brought it on themselves. Hosea married a prostitute (see Hosea 1:2). Jeremiah wore a back-bending oxen yoke (see Jeremiah 27:2). Isaiah "walked around naked and barefoot" for three years (Isaiah 20:2-3). Ezekiel "out-follyed" all the prophets by baking his bread over a pile of human excrement (see Ezekiel 4:12).[1]

Perhaps the apostle Paul had the prophets in mind when he wrote his first letter to the church at Corinth. Writing to a Christian community riddled with elitism and arrogance, Paul claimed to be exhibit A of holy folly. In sharp contrast to the "super apostles"—those ultraslick, dashing, polished, and eloquent spiritual leaders who were wooing the church—Paul ironically proclaimed, "We are fools for Christ. . . . We have become the scum of the earth" (1 Corinthians 4:10, 13, NIV), or as *The Message* puts it, "potato peelings from the culture's kitchen."

Nearly four hundred years after Paul, just as Christians were achieving personal comfort and social respectability, a group of countercultural believers fled the comforts of noisy streets and cozy church buildings. They moved into the desert, building small huts, weaving baskets for the poor, memorizing Scripture, wearing ragged clothes, eating rough bread and oil, engaging in contemplative prayer and spiritual warfare, and practicing radical compassion with unlimited hospitality. And that was only the beginning of a legacy of other holy fools who followed in their footsteps.[2]

A young man named Moling, a seventh-century Irish holy fool, had such Christlike love for lepers that he developed a ministry of caring for their physical needs, even to the point of wiping the snot from their running noses.

Christiana, a young woman living in medieval France, developed a deep aversion to unpleasant body odors. Nevertheless, she felt compelled to bring the love of Christ to peasants with poor hygiene. As she bound their wounds, she avoided vomiting by frequently bolting outside for fresh air. Christiana continued her ministry to hygienically challenged peasants throughout her life.

A young man named Francis came to Christ and promptly cast away all his possessions (and his father's too). He walked barefoot (and buck naked at least once), kissed lepers, and rebuilt a dilapidated church building on the outskirts of town. We call him a saint; his neighbors called him "*Pazzo!*"—madman.

In Russia during the sixteenth century, a *yurodivi* (the Russian word for "holy fool") named Basil scandalized and enraged respectable church people by tripping the most "righteous" church members as they entered the church, throwing stones at the homes of rich people who ignored the poor, and bathing the feet of prostitutes and demoniacs with his tears.

In the late 1800s, a forty-year-old single woman named Mary Slessor left her conventional church in Scotland and ventured into the heart of western Africa. After mastering the language and learning the culture, she spent the rest of her life in the jungle adopting unwanted babies, protecting battered women, and warding off enraged hippos and tribal chiefs.

About the same time, a young man named Hudson Taylor, a missionary in China, scandalized his respectable Christian friends by shaving his head—everything except the long, braided pigtail worn by the Chinese men of his day. He also wore the traditional Chinese pajama-like clothing and ate with chopsticks. We consider him a paragon of cross-cultural engagement; his own mission board deemed him an extremist.

I must confess, at least initially, these people irked me. Some of their antics qualified for a "spirituality of the weird." What's the point of weaving baskets in the desert, wiping snot from lepers' noses, or walking around buck naked? Is it really commendable to throw stones at houses? If body odors disgust you, perhaps it's time to take a "spiritual gifts inventory" and find a ministry that matches your unique temperament. How could these people serve as spiritual role models to me?

At least that was my initial response. At times these radical saints still bewilder me, but in the past ten years I've also developed a strange fascination with them. They didn't give neat formulas or pat answers for the journey in Christ. They didn't "settle" my spiritual life. Instead, like a strong wind rushing through dead leaves, they unsettled and scattered the dry fragments in my heart.

I noticed that every holy fool fit a certain profile—a profile that stood in marked contrast to the sad state of my spiritual life.

1. **The holy fools had passion.** Unlike me, the shocking believers in this stream of Christian spirituality were anything but mild; instead, they were excessive—excessively in love with God. All of them were willing to play the fool to follow Christ. All of them were willing to let the message of Christ "have the run of the house" in their lives (Colossians 3:16, *The Message*). I was busy serving Jesus, but I couldn't say I was living passionately for him. Somehow in the midst of doing stuff for Jesus, I had disconnected my heart from Jesus.

2. **The holy fools exuded "messy" spirituality.** Most of my previous mentors were models of spiritual neatness and order. For instance, when I was in junior high I remember spotting a huge billboard advertising the slick spirituality of a "decent" Christian family. The billboard contained a family of four—father, mother, boy, girl—who confidently displayed spiritual tidiness. Father and son were dressed neatly in a suit and tie, their hair slicked down with a shiny, greasy petroleum prod-

uct (probably our favorite brand—Lucky Tiger). The mother and daughter wore conservative dresses, their hair tucked straight and crisp. All four of them folded their hands in prayer as they gazed off into the heavenly realms. The caption told us their secret: "The Family That Prays Together Stays Together."[3]

The billboard's implications were clear. To be a Christian—or at least a churchgoer—implied respectability, cleanliness, conventionality. Christians are nice, decent, mild human beings who reinforce the status quo. I was trying hard to be *that* kind of Christian, but after twenty years, my spiritual life was unraveling. I was a tight, tidy, pompous Christian bore.

As I met the holy fools, I encountered another approach to the spiritual journey in Christ. They were anything but orderly, conventional, or even "appropriate." They didn't care about appearing "spiritually mature" or "religiously suave." They knew that spiritual growth is like giving birth: It's a painful, inconvenient, and messy process. This leads to some unpredictable conclusions: The sign of progress is not laughter but the gift of tears; the best ministry is to be silent with God; the best deeds are hidden from sight; the path to spiritual power is through our weakness; freedom comes from total surrender. The Lucky Tiger family had everything laid out so neat and clean. In sharp contrast, the holy fools were a long way from the family on the billboard; instead, they were countercultural, disorderly, shocking, and wild. They certainly weren't tidy, pompous Christian bores.

3. **The holy fools liked messy people.** They never flinched from engaging the culture around them. Instead, they strategically dwelled on the margins of society so they could embrace other marginal strugglers. I, on the other

hand, had entrenched myself behind the cozy walls of my Christian ghetto, feverishly impressing clean, religious people. The holy fools engaged the dregs of their culture—prostitutes, demoniacs, the poor, the insane, the lepers, and the disabled. Their mission was to love misfits, people untouched by the respectable and righteous church people of their day. And they wanted to awaken the church to this mission as well.

4. **The holy fools were always in trouble.** With their excessive passion, their messy spirituality, and their sketchy friends, the holy fools weren't very popular. Good people mocked them. The good people's children threw stones at them. Public authorities locked them up. Church leaders branded them extremists. Average churchgoers wanted to wring their necks. In a church culture based on self-righteous separation and a cool and passionless spirituality, the holy fools just didn't fit.

The Ultimate Holy Fool

As I continued to engage this motley crew of holy fools, I began to notice a distinct resemblance to another very famous holy fool—Jesus. In my clean and tidy Christian world, we never classified Jesus as a fool. Instead, Jesus was the nice, well-mannered, conventional CEO of the slick Lucky Tiger people. But as I read the Gospels through the lens of holy folly, I discovered that Jesus was not a Lucky Tiger kind of guy. Yes, Jesus was and is the eternal Son of God, the perfect radiance of the Father's glory (see Hebrews 1:3). Yes, Jesus' teaching sparkled with wit, wisdom, and sanity. But the more I read the Gospels, the more I concluded that Jesus also fit the profile of a holy fool, and not just any holy fool, but the ultimate holy fool.

For starters, Jesus had a messy approach to the spiritual journey. Consider his birth. Theologians call it the Incarnation, which is a nice way to describe the wild story of God's shocking and messy descent into our bloody brokenness. The early Greek intellectuals were repulsed by this gross and indecent hallmark of Christian belief. I read an obscure Greek philosopher who ridiculed the Incarnation by asking sarcastically, "How can one admit the divine should become an embryo, that after his birth he is put in swaddling clothes, that he is soiled with blood and bile and worse things yet."[4]

Soiled with blood and bile and worse things? What bad form. Surely a proper God, a really smart God, a slick and impressive God, could think of a better entrance into the world. How utterly messy, ragged, and foolish!

Then consider his messy approach to death. There's nothing quite as ragged or shocking as a crucifixion. Death by crucifixion was not only bloody and noisy and obscene (decent people didn't even mention the word), it also stigmatized the crucified as a troublesome rebel and a low-life loser.[5] God redeeming the world by dying on a cross? The "logic" of a Savior dying on a cross, an instrument of execution reserved for common criminals, seems beyond inappropriate and illogical—even downright nonsense. Only a powerful, wonder-working, enemy-smashing God can really save people. But God on a cross, a Messiah who became vulnerable, a Savior of suffering love? How stupid can you get?

During my first pastorate I met a fiery fifteen-year-old foster boy named Jimmy who clearly understood the scandal of the Cross. Jimmy wasn't his birth name. Born on the streets of Chile, Jimmy lost his mother early in life, and his father, a drunken and enraged man, used to beat Jimmy and his sister. So when most children were adding two plus two and eating peanut butter sandwiches, Jimmy was learning to run and fight—fighting his father, fighting corrupt cops who despised runaway children, fighting other street kids for scraps of food in hotel Dumpsters.

One day a nice couple from Minnesota adopted Jimmy and his sister, but Jimmy couldn't stop fighting. He fought so hard that his new parents released him to the state and he was, at last, delivered to the home of Leon and Nancy, committed Christians, members of my first church, and foster parents to ten boys at a time. Jimmy helped make punch for our coffee fellowship hour, and he seemed interested in God . . . until we discussed the Cross. As I explained the last days of Jesus' life and how he chose to die a painful death on a Roman cross for our sins, Jimmy's eyes widened with shock and horror. With a look of utter disgust, Jimmy asked, "Why would anyone do something that stupid? Jesus is a fool!" Then Jimmy proceeded to tell a more suitable ending to the story: Instead of dying, Jesus pulls out an AK-47 assault rifle and guns down his enemies. Rather than the "victory" of his crucifixion, Jesus, the big man with the fast gun, stands victorious over a pile of bloody, bullet-ridden corpses. "Yeah," Jimmy concluded, nodding his head in approval, "now that would make Jesus cool and not a fool."

"Well, Jimmy," I remember responding, "that sure is interesting. Um, that's not the typical answer I hear from the church kids around here, but I appreciate your honesty." I still appreciate Jimmy's honesty. He was more honest than many believers. We wear crosses around our necks and sing sentimental songs about the cross. We invite Jesus into our lives and our churches, but we let him stay only if he behaves like the nice family on the billboard. "Keep your hair plastered down with Lucky Tiger," we tell Jesus, "and don't start knocking over tables or bleeding on a cross.

And please don't drip any blood on the new carpet. Be decent, Jesus. Be appropriate and well-mannered."

According to Jimmy (and the entire New Testament), however, there is an edge to Jesus and his death on a cross—a shocking, brutal, and horrible edge. The cross is messy and inappropriate. It looks downright stupid. If God really wanted to save the planet, he couldn't have picked a more ridiculous instrument.

The biblical writers plowed into and even reveled in the irony of it all. Through the weakness of the Cross, God displayed power, canceling our debt and disarming "the spiritual rulers and authorities . . . by his victory over them on the cross" (Colossians 2:15). For the early Christians, this notion was deliciously subversive and ironic. The wisest and strongest and bravest couldn't concoct a plan to cancel our debt, disarm the powers, reconcile us with God, and heal broken hearts and a broken planet (see 1 Corinthians 1:21). But God, like a grand master chess player, used one unpredictable but masterful move—the Cross—to put all the pieces in place, confounding the powers of darkness and sweeping us into his victory over sin and death and hell. Through the foolishness of the Cross, God displayed wisdom, resolving the greatest philosophical, ethical, and relational dilemma in the universe: how to reconcile a holy God with sinful humanity. In doing so, he embraced lost creatures as sons and daughters and brought healing to a broken universe (see Romans 8:22-24).

Then consider Jesus' messy, unconventional teachings. I began to notice the sharp edges to his spirituality. Jesus is filled with surprises. Guess who gets blessed with outrageous happiness? According to Jesus, it's the poor in spirit, the mourners, the persecuted (see Matthew 5:3-12). Guess who receives the healing touch of God? It's not the healthy or the righteous; it's sick people—distorted, broken, and bleeding sinners who desperately need mercy (see Matthew 9:9-13). Guess how the father responds to his rebellious son who wasted his life and ate pig slop? He sprints toward him, embraces him, kisses him, and gives him a big, fat, juicy steak (see Luke 15:11-24). Guess who went home justified before God? Surprise, it's not the guy who sat up front and prayed the long, eloquent prayers; it's the loser in the back pew who, with tears streaming down his face, doesn't feel worthy to step through the church doors (see Luke 18:9-14).

Like the holy fools throughout history, Jesus' behavior opened him to the mockery of others. After his first public sermon, a group of religious leaders tried to shove him over a cliff (see Luke 4:29). His closest relatives labeled him a half-baked, excessive fool (see Mark 3:21). The Bible scholars of his day claimed Jesus was possessed not only by a demon but by the "prince of demons" (Mark 3:22).

The religious leaders had good reason to question Jesus' approach. To start with, they argued, look at the people he embraced: prostitutes, lepers, tax collectors, uncouth fishermen, and "sinners." He allowed a woman of questionable character to barge into his presence and sensuously[6] wipe his feet with her tears and her hair (see Luke 7:36-50). Lepers begged for healing and he broke social etiquette by tenderly touching them (see Mark 1:40-45). When he met a wild-eyed demoniac, wrapped in chains and howling in the tombs, Jesus performed a countercultural act by addressing and then healing the man (see Mark 5:1-20). Much to the shock of decent people everywhere, Jesus invited himself to dinner with a notorious sawed-off, greedy rip-off artist named Zaccheus (see Luke 19:1-10).

I concluded that the Gospels were the story of God's holy folly, the sheer foolishness of a God who does outlandish things for unlikely people. It wasn't nice and proper. Jesus was about as well mannered as a tornado sweeping through your living room, violently picking up and tossing everything in its path—sofas, chairs, tables, lamps, even the carpeting—until nothing remains except the firm concrete underneath your feet. Which, once again, is precisely the role of Jesus and every Christlike fool. The holy fools started to gut my heart of a smug, tidy, pompous spirituality until I stood squarely on God's mercy.

A Strange Way to Wake Up

It dawned on me that Jesus and his ragtag band of holy fools were on a spiritual journey radically different from mine. I had achieved decency, order, and respectability, and I associated with like-minded people. The holy fools disrupted all of that. They rattled me. Through their messy and unconventional approach to faith in Christ, these ragged saints offered me a "ministry of awakening." My faith had grown cold; they wanted to light a fire deep within my heart. I was coasting on my spiritual journey; they kicked me in the rear end. I recall the Southern writer Flannery O'Connor explaining why she wrote such extreme, shocking, and even grotesque short stories. "To the hard of hearing," she said, "you have to shout, and for the almost blind you draw large and startling figures." The holy fools were shouting and scribbling to my nearly deaf and blind soul.

And this certainly wasn't the suave spirituality of the billboard family. Holy fools didn't lull the faithful with visions of sweetness and decency; they shocked the faithful with the surprising edge of Jesus' path. They viewed spiritual complacency as the greatest danger to the Christian journey. So everything they did was directed at awakening and startling men and women whose hearts had grown numb, dull, and apathetic.

But I also notice that authentic holy fools never reveled in their novelty or extremism. They didn't aim at a cutting-edge lifestyle; they merely embarked on a journey with Jesus—and they allowed it to change everything. They drank in the pure gospel long enough for it to permanently alter their brains. The gospel threw them off balance; it made them drunk with God until they staggered with a holy passion. They became extremists, but theirs was an extremism of love, an immoderate, extraordinary, uncalculated pursuit of love for God and their neighbors.

Compared to the holy fools, how stiff and stuffy my spirituality appears. How correct but how tepid. While I dutifully follow my Bible reading plan, they allowed God's Word to break their hearts wide open. While I talk about witnessing to my neighbors, they actually invited them into their lives and their homes. While I analyze contemplative prayer, they moved into the silent forests and practiced it. With their playful antics, they are in the process of subverting my spiritual arrogance.

Encounters with Contemporary Holy Fools

All the holy fools give me the same invitation: Wake up! But they don't offer that invitation through trite words or predictable methods. Instead, with unexpected and playful twists, they penetrate my normal defenses and subvert my normal expectations, awakening my heart.

I'll never forget a contemporary holy fool named Roberta. Roberta's family didn't fit the profile of the "perfect church people." They followed a ragged path to church and to Jesus. Roberta's dad had recently dropped dead from a heart attack. Church had never been an option in her mom's spiritual outlook. She had too many questions and too much anger toward God to fit into your typical small group. But her grieving mom, Roberta, and her older brother started coming to our church, and we started loving them. Roberta's mom kept showing up, bringing the kids, learning, growing, questioning, and finding some answers, until best of all, she found Jesus (or Jesus found her). Roberta's mom is feisty and smart and funny, and we love having her. She asks hard questions and won't settle for cheap answers, but she keeps seeking and growing.

Anyway, one fine Sunday morning we started worship with the children's choir dressed in white shirts and red vests singing a lovely introit. Roberta was front and center, singing loudly. She's a wonderful kid, but on that particular morning she kept getting the song wrong. The words from her mouth didn't match what all the other kids were singing. Roberta grew more and more frustrated until she just gave up and sat on the floor, leaning against our wooden lectern. The lectern started to wobble until it finally plummeted off the altar area and smacked right into the middle of the Communion table, crushing the shiny silver Communion trays. Our nice children's choir kept singing the lovely introit as two ushers scrambled to set up the lectern.

Everyone pretended it didn't happen, but for the rest of the service I kept staring at the silver cross on top of the Communion tray. When the lectern fell on that beautiful tray, it crushed the pretty silver cross. At a few points in the service I discreetly tried to straighten the silver cross until I finally gave up. I just left it twisted and flattened. And then it hit me: We try so hard to make our worship pretty and peaceful. And certainly I'm in favor of beauty (God is, after all, a God of beauty). But when Jesus shows up, he reminds us that our worship is beautiful because God became ugly; it's peaceful because Jesus endured agony; it's nice and clean because the lovely Son of God spilled his blood all over the raw earth.

Thank you, Roberta. On a nice Sunday morning you led me in worship. You ushered me onto holy ground. You created the most profound Communion service I've ever experienced. You are a holy fool for Christ.

Over a ten-year period God has used surprising mentors like Alan, Ezekiel, Paul, Moling, Francis, Mary, and of course Jesus to stir, disrupt, and awaken my heart. This is the story of my unexpected journey with the holy fools. In particular it's the story of how God awakened me in key areas of my life: vulnerability, compassion, spiritual discipline, and spiritual passion.

Twelve years ago as I sat hunched over the steering wheel of the church van, a broken and pierced man, I had no idea that God was taking me on a new journey. It started as an awakening to my own vulnerability. As God awakened my heart, he began to subvert and demolish my walls of self-righteousness. And strangely enough, it all started with the creeping awareness of a virus that was threatening to suck the spiritual life right out of me if I didn't act quickly.

QUESTIONS FOR REFLECTION

What is the level of your passion for Christ? Do you do things for Jesus while your heart has disconnected from him?

Does your spiritual journey in Christ constantly take turns that surprise you? Or is your journey entirely predictable and mild?

Do you love "messy people"? Who are the misfits (besides yourself) you are loving in Jesus' name?

Have you ever been in trouble for your faith in Christ? When was the last time someone claimed that you, your small group, or your entire church was spiritually "drunk with God" until you "staggered with a holy passion"?

Do you know someone who is a contemporary holy fool? What are the potential dangers and gifts of holy folly?

AWAKENING TO A LIFE
OF COMPASSION

CHAPTER 2

Subverting Self-Righteousness

I do not like seriousness. I think it is irreligious. . . . The man who takes himself too seriously is the man who makes an idol of everything.

G. K. CHESTERTON

SHORTLY AFTER I GAVE my heart to Jesus, I became a well-known religious jerk. At the time, I merely considered myself "on fire for God." During my summer vacation I spent four hours every afternoon memorizing large portions of the Bible—which I spewed on people at unsuspecting moments. In my free time I hung out with "real Christians" at a "real church." I witnessed to my family members, starting from the premise that they were clearly on the road to eternal damnation—and I was okay with that. I did all these things with the utmost religious conviction, sincerity, and sense of rightness.

After about six months of this newfound religious fervor, one of my sisters just couldn't take it anymore. After dinner, while she did the dishes and I memorized the Sermon on the Mount, she asked if we could take a little stroll around our neighborhood. I didn't get a chance to witness to her because she did all the talking. And as I recall, her monologue went something like this: "You call yourself a Christian, huh? Well, let me tell you, since you 'came to Jesus,' you have become one of the most unhelpful and unpleasant people I've ever met. You show blatant disrespect for Mom and Dad. You don't do any chores like the rest of us. You never talk to us; you just preach at us. You talk about God's love, but you don't even like us anymore. Worst of all, you never laugh with us or have fun with us. I don't know what you've experienced with Jesus Christ; all I know is that I used to like you a lot more before you accepted Jesus. You've become mean and kind of creepy. I can't tell you to give up this Jesus stuff (although it sort of looks like a bunch of religious hooey), but could you just act nicer?"

Not that I reformed overnight, but eventually that conversation with my sister helped me in my spiritual growth more than the forty-five-minute Bible-based sermons I was hearing week after week. In a six-minute "devotional," she exposed a deadly virus that often infects religious people and masquerades as true spirituality. It's called self-righteousness, and off and on throughout my life, I've caught the virus.

Jesters in the Church: The Role of Holy Fools

I didn't know it at the time, but my sister was not only doing me a favor, she was also acting like a true holy fool. As I began to walk with the holy fools later in life, I saw them expose and then puncture the pompous, overblown, puffed-up balloon of my spiritual smugness. Like my sister, the holy fools confronted me and other "good Christian people" with a simple message: "I don't care how often you show up at church. I don't care how often you quote the Bible. I don't care how 'right' you act or how 'rightly' you hold to the truth. Did it ever occur to you that your arrogance, spiritual pomposity, and self-righteousness make you dead wrong? While taking God with the utmost seriousness, why don't you do us all a huge favor by laughing at yourself and joining the rest of this messy, flawed group of sinners called the human race?"

I discovered that some of the greatest holy fools acted just like my sister, although unlike her and like the court jesters of their day, the holy fools sweetened their blunt critique with disarming doses of humor, wit, buffoonery, and exaggeration. Perhaps the greatest holy fool in this regard was a sixteenth-century Russian named Symeon. After spending his early years in contemplative prayer, Symeon reengaged society by declaring, "I am going to mock the world." Symeon never set out to mock people made in the image of God; he merely mocked the pretentiousness of spiritual arrogance and smugness.

So Symeon played the fool in the full sense of the word, bringing a lighthearted, playful approach to his spiritual life. On the way into worship services, Symeon snuck up behind and tripped the most "righteous" church members of his day. On other occasions, this alleged man of God limped, hopped, or dragged himself along on his rear end. When the best and brightest church members fasted on special feast days (and let everyone know about it), Symeon mocked their smug self-righteousness by standing on a busy street corner munching on a chunk of sausage. He further shocked the righteous by consorting with the marginalized members of society—drunks, demoniacs, the poor, the homeless, and prostitutes, whom he called "my girlfriends."

Mixing playful buffoonery with spirituality scandalized the righteous—which was precisely the point. Naturally, in our context, tripping the self-righteous and munching on sausages may not get the right point across. We could wind up acting like an equally self-righteous—and obnoxious—band of "hypocrite police." The ancient holy fools always had a clear goal: By their bizarre and comical "jesterizing," the holy fools mocked every form of self-righteousness and spiritual arrogance. They laughed, danced, tripped people, and chewed sausages, all in an attempt to expose, disrupt, and deconstruct the arrogance that often lurks beneath our spiritual lives. Holy fools like Symeon and my sister have brought a radical message to me and to good church people: Lighten up! Yes, take God with the utmost seriousness, but don't take yourself so seriously. Don't act so intolerably stiff, and don't pretend you're so damn[1] righteous. Laugh at yourself, because your stiff, smug self-righteousness is killing us all.

The Ugly Facade of Self-Righteousness

Throughout my life I've noticed that these jesterlike holy fools do me a huge favor. Self-righteousness stinks! Shortly after my introduction to the holy fools, I watched the movie *Chocolat*. It weaves the story of a single woman who moves into a small, provincial, "Christian" town in France. She scandalizes the respectable church people by opening a chocolate shop during Lent, when every kind of sweet is strictly prohibited. The shop, complete with Mayan and pagan artifacts, creates a swirl of controversy. The mayor, a stern and devout man who upholds the church's moral teaching and views himself with utmost seriousness, leads a crusade to close the chocolate shop. He never laughs or dances, but ultimately the joke will be on him. One night, after the shop has closed, the mayor breaks into the window display, devouring large pieces of rich, dark delicacies until he can't even budge, chocolate smeared on his face and hands. Without a holy fool to derail his runaway arrogance, the mayor made a train wreck of his spiritual life.

Beginning a decade ago, the holy fools started breaking into my comfortable existence. Initially their approach stretched me, but it began to dawn on me that they were also filling in the gaps of my experience. So I hungered for more—reading biographies and writings of these quirky Christ followers. It finally got to the point that I knew I *needed* the faith-stretching perspective of these men and women who were not like me. These holy fools began to expose the ugly pride that lurks behind my mask of devotion.

Even my diligence in the spiritual disciplines can become a badge of honor and superiority. I'm committed—what's wrong with everyone else? I get it—why can't they? If people interrupt my prayer times, I get crabby. (*Would you all just shut up? Can't you see I'm contemplating over here?*) My busyness with church meetings isolates me from lost people, who are no longer real names and faces but just a general category. I resent people who can't comprehend "real" worship. They're too stuffy or too loose; they're never just right—like me. I'm impressed when others label me (quite accurately, I might add) a "spiritual leader" or a "godly person." I started to admit that the German philosopher Friedrich Nietzsche had a point about my spiritual journey: My "goodness" can easily serve as a slick front for my raw will to power over others.

But the holy fools taught me that self-righteousness repulsed Jesus more than it repulsed Nietzsche. In Jesus' life and teaching I began to find an unrelenting assault on the smug arrogance behind our spirituality. For instance, I've always loved the parable of the Prodigal Son because it's my story. I identify with the younger son's rebellion, and I yearn for the father's embrace. But with fresh eyes I recognized the story of my life in the elder brother. When the younger brother finally returned from his ragged journey, the elder brother appears exactly where we expect him—out "in the fields working" (Luke 15:25). He stands at his post. He's dutiful, obedient, and respectable. He has always been that way, never straying, never leaving his post. Just like me, he has tried so hard to be the good son.

But don't be fooled, Jesus and the holy fools warn me. Lying just beneath the respectable veneer, my "good son" routine seethes with all the symptoms of the self-righteousness virus:

1. **Self-centeredness.** "You never gave *me* a party," he whines to his father (see Luke 15:29). "What about *me*? What about *my* party? Where's the fatted calf for *me*? Who cares about my brother; I want a party—a nice, warm, comfortable party—for just me and my friends. I don't get it. He wasted his life and now you're wasting the fatted calf on him? How about a little attention for *me*?" Like the older son, I'm often addicted to self-pity.

2. **Self-deception.** "All these years I've slaved for you and never once refused to do a single thing you told me to" (verse 29). Rubbish! Yes, he has worked like a dog, but he certainly hasn't always obeyed. He's defying his father right now. His father begs him to join the celebration, serving as the assistant host, mingling with the guests, filling wine glasses, rejoicing with his father, and embracing his younger brother. But the good son stands outside and pouts. In the same way, self-righteousness blinds me to my own sin.

3. **Contemptuousness.** Notice the contempt and disgust toward his younger brother: "This son of yours [he can't stomach the fact that it's his brother too] comes back after squandering your money on prostitutes" (verse 30). Who said anything about prostitutes? Apparently the elder son added this touching detail to put the worst possible spin on his brother's actions. My older sister was right: My conversion made me dislike ragged people. My spiritual "achievements" can slowly drain mercy out of my heart and fill me with contempt.

4. **Joylessness.** In Luke 15 Jesus piles on three stories that shimmer with God's joy. By the end of the stories everyone parties, laughing until they hurt, raising and clinking glasses of wine, munching on hamburgers, dancing to the flute and the lyre—everyone, that is, except the good son. Like the good son, I'm in danger of becoming what Mark Twain called "a good man—in the worst sense of the word."

Commenting on the elder brother, the German theologian Helmut Thielicke wrote, "There are no festivals in this life, but only the tedious, tiresome, though highly serious monotony. . . . There is a kind of obedience that has about it a mildewed, numbing lack of freshness and vitality that never makes a person really happy. There are plenty of 'good people' whose religion never makes them really warm and happy. . . . There is no concealing the fact that sometimes God becomes boring to them."[2]

Through a process of reading the Gospels, finding the radical message of Jesus on a new level, and reading the perspective of the holy fools, I slowly concluded that I needed an unrelenting assault on my spiritual smugness. Self-righteousness was like a voracious tapeworm in my spiritual life, consuming everything I put in my soul, leaving me famished and gaunt. As long as the worm is in my system, spiritual feeding—e.g., Bible study, worship, prayer, good works—merely feeds the worm of spiritual pride. Spiritual disciplines, rather than making me soft and tender like the waiting father, merely reinforce the condescending, joyless elder brother spirit. Someone needs to pierce our armor with the dagger of truth. For God's sake, for my sake, for our sake as the people of Jesus Christ, someone needs to name and dislocate our spiritual strutting and posing.

Enter the holy fools. Historically, especially in the Russian version of the yurodivi, holy fools rarely appear when the church suffers persecution or hardship; instead, holy fools appear when the church wallows in its own smug, comfortable, and exclusive "success." Then the holy fools arise to expose the tapeworm and elder brother in all of us. They dare to "speak the truth in love" (Ephesians 4:15), piercing our armor of arrogance.

Unfortunately, most of what passes for truth telling or confrontation in Christian community is really just meanness cloaked in God talk. A few weeks ago, for instance, I received a letter in which someone accused me of all manner of debauchery, corruption, and licentiousness. The letter had a Long Island postmark, but I have no idea who sent it—or why. "Are you for real?" he asked. "I have never seen such depths of greed, narcissism, selfishness, lust, spiritual immaturity, hard-heartedness . . . ." (There was more, but I think you get the point.) Initially, I thought, *Wow, this guy missed a few sins, but otherwise he knows me pretty well.* He signed it anonymously as "your brother in Christ," but for some reason I couldn't feel the family love.

In contrast, I saw that God's holy fools rarely took mean swipes or frontal assaults on people. They rarely clubbed people with truth. Because they loved deeply, they always seemed to utilize two subversive practices to confront self-righteousness: truth with a smile and truth with a twist.

Truth with a Smile

The holy fools possessed a quality that was often lacking in highly religious people like me: lighthearted humor. Actually, their entire approach to the spiritual life was often marked by a touch of levity. I loved discovering the story of Romuald, a largely unknown eleventh-century monk who exuded a shocking jesterlike cheerfulness. His biographers called it *alacritas*, or "spiritual bounce."[3] For instance, when evil spirits descended on him, Romuald simply laughed them away, choosing to exorcise with satire and jest: "Look, I'm ready; come on!" he shouted at the demons. "Let's see your power, if that's what it is. Or are you really powerless? Are you defeated? Don't you have some secret weapon to bring out against God's little servant?" I laughed when I pictured the image of a gentle monk, slapping his chest, taunting the powers of hell with words that might have sounded like this: "Yo, demons, you want a piece of me? Oh, wow, so that's your best shot. You call that temptation? Bring it on, you twits."

One time a thief broke into Romuald's monastery, and the brothers promptly "arrested" him. I would expect most spiritual leaders would have sternly lectured the thief. Not Romuald. He treated him with good-natured humor. "I just don't know what to do with such a wicked man," Romuald pondered out loud. "Shall we tear out his eyes? But then he won't be able to see. Shall we cut off his hand? But then he won't work anymore and will probably die of hunger. Shall we chop off his foot? Then he couldn't walk. Why don't you take him inside and give him lunch?" After feeding and caring for the man, Romuald "admonished him with sweet words."

Certainly, the holy fools could be serious, but they also knew how to play and dance—and how I need to laugh and dance. Without humor and levity, my spirituality turns serious, sour, grim, and eventually even cruel. About midway into my discovery of the holy fools, I reread the following words from Blaise Pascal's *Pensée*: "Men never do evil so completely and cheerfully as when they do it from religious conviction." I realized that a certain form of so-called religious conviction made me stop dancing, playing, juggling, skipping, and loving. I no longer marveled and delighted in God's grace. Finally I was starting to understand G. K. Chesterton's dire warning: "I do not like seriousness. I think it is irreligious. . . . The man who takes himself too seriously is the man who makes an idol of everything."[4]

Unfortunately, I had to admit that I shared a common trait with tyrants, warlords, and a mafioso—we all refuse to laugh at ourselves, and we won't let others laugh at us either. For instance, when NPR commentator Andrei Codrescu ridiculed the concept of the Rapture, calling it "crap" and arguing that the world would improve with the "evaporation" of millions who believed this, Christians were grim in their outrage. Codrescu received hate mail and death threats (in Christian love, of course). So while NPR apologized, Mr. Codrescu became more entrenched in his position that we're intellectually naive.[5]

But under the tutelage of the holy fools, I started to take a different approach. While holding ardently to the truth of Scripture, why not respond with a smile? What if we upended Mr. Codrescu with humor and wit? How about, "Mr. Codrescu, thank you for mentioning our 'crap.' Hey, as long as I haven't been vaporized yet, could we talk about it over a cup of coffee?" Clearly, people in the holy fool tradition strive for something more creative, witty, and just plain fun than hate mail.

Truth with a Twist

My friend Denis Haack pointed out to me that psychologist Jean Piaget identified a teaching technique called disequilibration. Piaget discovered that all of us—children and adults—are most challenged to learn when a teacher disrupts and upends our normal assumptions. Someone throws us off balance. Surprise, irony, questions, challenges, stories, and stark images—the holy fools utilized all these tools to throw us off balance, creating a sense of disequilibration for a redemptive purpose.

A few years ago my friend Ryan became my spiritual jester. As I whined about the lack of intimacy in my life, Ryan responded with soothing words: "You know, Matt, I just don't understand because you're a really nice person."

"Well," I said humbly, "I guess most people would say that I'm pretty nice."

"No, you're *really* nice. And you're not only nice, but you're very loving. So I just don't understand why you're having a problem with intimacy in your life."

"Yeah, I agree, it doesn't make sense, does it?" I said.

"I mean, you practically exude love. Everyone knows that."

"I guess you're right, Ryan."

And then, with the twist of a holy fool, Ryan casually leaned back in his chair and said, "Hmm, I just wonder though . . ."

"Wonder about what?"

"Well, now that we've amassed irrefutable evidence for your niceness, I wonder if your 'niceness' serves as a mechanism for self-protection? Hmm . . . maybe some of it isn't love at all. Maybe some of it is even a narcissistic fantasy. And maybe that's why you have so little intimacy in your life."

After five years of friendship I knew that Ryan spoke in love, but his words still pierced clean through my cloak of false spirituality. Ryan became my personal holy fool. In effect, Ryan was saying, "Matt, I'm for you so much that I'll expose and then disrupt your spiritual pride. I'll throw your life off balance. I'll tell you that you're really buck naked, and you desperately need Christ to clothe you with his grace." Like the ancient jesters and holy fools, with a surprise attack, Ryan stripped through my layers of niceness, cut through my armor of "spiritual maturity," and offered my smug soul a taste of truth and healing.

I found the self-righteousness–smashing twist of holy folly in the Bible as well. For instance, I noted that after King David had solidified his kingdom, his spiritual life slid into the cesspool. Lust, adultery, murder, self-deception—David was drowning in a thick soup of sewage, but he didn't know it. Then his mentor, Nathan the prophet, came to David and shared a shocking story. A rich man needed lamb stew for his houseguests, but rather than using a lamb from his massive ranch, he went next door and grabbed the family pet from his poor neighbor. Naturally, David howled in protest. Oh, the injustice and immorality of it all. As Nathan drew David into the story and as David worked himself into a frenzy of moral outrage, Nathan pointed a bony finger at David and quietly said, "You are that man!" Once again, a holy fool dished out truth with a twist, surprise, and disequilibration. To his credit, David listened to Nathan, and God softened his heart (see 2 Samuel 12).

I noticed, of course, that Jesus himself was a master of dishing out truth with a twist. The Pharisees had earned the prize for religious seriousness. Like me, they followed the rules. They believed the right things. They even tithed on everything in their spice rack (see Matthew 23:23). Their spiritual practices were impeccably in balance. But just like the holy fools, Jesus used humor, exaggeration, sarcasm, and wit to throw them off balance. In his unrelenting assault on their self-righteousness,

Jesus piled on one stark and shocking picture after another (see Matthew 23):

- "You cross land and sea to make one convert, and then you turn that person into twice the child of hell you yourselves are!" (verse 15)

- "Blind guides! You strain your water so you won't accidentally swallow a gnat, but you swallow a camel!" (verse 24)

- "You are so careful to clean the outside of the cup and the dish, but inside you are filthy—full of greed and self-indulgence!" (verse 25)

With each of these individuals—Ryan, Nathan, and Jesus—I saw that a holy fool dared to speak the truth with a twist, slicing through a layer of pride and spiritual deception. I discovered my need for a holy fool to enter my life and knock me off balance, strip my heart of self-righteousness, and propel me on a journey to spiritual reality.

The Poison of Self-Righteousness

For some people it's tempting to view self-righteousness as a peculiar penchant of religious people or maybe just evangelical Christians. But the problem runs much deeper. Self-righteousness lurks in every human heart. I'm often shocked to hear sophisticated, enlightened, "open-minded" fellow New Yorkers speak with inexcusable ignorance and unsparing contempt for entire groups of people—rural Americans, Southerners, evangelical Christians, theists, the "uneducated" (i.e., those who didn't attend an East Coast school), or political conservatives. The comments seethe with a withering disdain. The brilliant Manhattan-based writer

Susan Sontag once confessed in her journal: "One of my strongest and most fully employed emotions: *contempt.* Contempt for others, contempt for myself."[6] The poison of self-righteousness has seeped into every human heart.

Self-righteousness even leaks into our use of humor. When the reporter Lance Morrow set out to write an article on the question of whether there was one universal, cross-cultural joke, he sent a query to news bureaus around the world—Moscow, Beijing, Tokyo, Sydney, New Delhi, Paris, Buenos Aires, and so on. It turns out that there is one universal joke that cuts across cultures. It's what Americans used to call the "dumb Polish joke." Growing up in Minnesota, we called it the "dumb Iowan joke." I never would have guessed they told jokes about Minnesotans. It's a joke based on self-righteous contempt for others. So the English tell Irish jokes. The Flemings have Walloon jokes. The people in Tokyo disdainfully mock those from Osaka. Even the inhabitants from the tiny island of Grenada (a mere 133 square miles) tell vicious jokes about people on the other side of the island. How sick can you get? According to Morrow, we need others so we can enjoy pouring contempt on them. Self-righteousness is an equal opportunity sin, cutting across cultures and creeds.[7]

According to the biblical story there is only one medicine strong enough to treat the poison of self-righteousness: the gospel. The gospel attacks the deadly infection of contempt for the other. At the heart of the gospel we hear this message: Christ died for our sins, and God chose us not based on our performance or our good deeds or our many excellent qualities or because we're a cut above other people. No, Christ died on the cross and God adopted us into his family because God is gracious and kind. It's an idea that's utterly radical and counterintuitive. "God showed his great love for us by sending Christ to die for us while we were still sinners" (Romans 5:8). God's grace permanently removes any possible grounds to stand before pure holiness and boast that I'm better than another human being. The ground truly is level at the foot of the cross. Nothing—not brilliance, heritage, money, education, achievements, race, religious effort—makes me more acceptable to God. As we apply and reapply the medicine of the gospel, it slowly heals the raging infection of self-righteousness.

Life after Self-Righteousness

Actually, I don't have any idea what it's like to have a life after self-righteousness, but I am discovering a spiritual life with far less smug arrogance and contempt toward ragged people. With regular encounters with holy fools, God has begun to strip the veneer of self-righteousness from my heart. As a result, I'm realizing I need to take myself and my own righteousness much less seriously.

Recently when my "brother in Christ" lambasted my character, the chemicals in my body kicked into a fight-or-flight response—and I wanted to fight. "How dare you accuse me of such sinful tendencies?" I wanted to protest. "How dare you attack me, a *senior* pastor of all things. Why don't you show yourself, you spiritual twit. I'd like to see your track record of righteousness." I was outraged and leaped to my own defense, duly noting my own righteousness.

To a lesser degree, that's how most of us react when we feel ignored, criticized, or slighted. We rush to defend our record of righteousness. But what if someone could deliver us from this incessant, immature need to defend our track record of righteousness? What if I could allow the truth in another's critique to penetrate my "armor of rightness"? What if I could be secure enough to rest in God's grace alone? Enter the holy fools. That's part of their ministry of awakening. As someone once commented, the holy fools "throw spitballs at and hurl catcalls at our presumed self-importance."[8]

I need the holy fools to enter my life on a daily basis, subverting my self-righteousness. This subversion provides an exquisite relief, like falling gently, naked and fearless, into a clear pool on a muggy summer afternoon. Ah, at long last, I can stop running and sweating and striving. I can fall into God's arms as the flawed, broken, sinful, ridiculous human being that I really am. In my nakedness and vulnerability, I've realized that only one thing can clothe me—the righteousness of Christ. "It is because of him that you are in Christ Jesus, who has become for us wisdom from God—that is, our righteousness, holiness and redemption," wrote the apostle Paul (1 Corinthians 1:30, NIV). To my delight, his righteousness is more than enough to cover my shame.

As I rest in God's grace, trusting in the righteousness of Christ alone, there have been two practical shifts in my approach to the spiritual life. First, by popping my bubble of self-righteousness and helping me take myself less seriously, the holy fools are teaching me to take God and his glory far more seriously. With their radically God-centered vision, they free me from my compulsion to be at the center of reality, strutting my ego and proving my righteousness. I'm starting to realize that the Bible constantly opens our spirits to a fresh, God-centered vision of his holiness (see Isaiah 40:12-31).

There's a common biblical phrase for taking God more seriously in our lives; it's called the fear of the Lord. Toward the end of his life, the apostle Peter, a man who knew the deep love of Jesus for sinners, nevertheless urged us to live before our Father with "reverent fear" (1 Peter 1:17). The fear of the Lord doesn't mean soul-destroying dread, because our Judge is also our Father. On the other hand, fear is the appropriate response when we meet something that is other, greater, stronger, fiercer than we are.

In my wife's hometown in the Rocky Mountains, you just might encounter a grizzly bear. You *will* take a grizzly bear with utmost seriousness. It could tear you to pieces and then eat you—or it could just rip off an arm. You take the bear seriously and you don't think about proving your point or defending your honor or meriting righteousness. You fear the grizzly because it is other; it is stronger than you. How much more so should we fear God, the source of holiness—a blazing center of pure holiness. When Peter met the holiness of Jesus (see Luke 5), he fell flat on his face and declared, "Depart from me, for I am a sinful man" (verse 8, NKJV). At that point in his life, Peter was not pondering or defending or declaring his own righteousness. In the presence of pure holiness, he fell flat on his face. When we stop worrying about our own righteousness, our focus shifts to God's righteousness.

Second, when I stop trying to prove my righteousness, it clears the way for true community. Community is impossible when I'm forever hankering to defend my point and my righteousness. A few weeks ago my friend Billy sent me a high-strung, angry, condescending e-mail. Billy seemed to be sending a clear message: *You are wrong and I am right so stop acting like an idiot*— or at least that was my initial impression. I immediately wrote a scathing and sarcastic reply, but right before I pushed the Send button, I stopped and asked myself a few questions: Do I always have to be right? Do I always have to defend myself? Do I always have to respond to an insult with an insult? Am I not acting like the older brother right now? Is there a better way? How can I reach out in love to Billy and build community?

What would Jesus, the holy fool, say to me? Maybe, "You're acting like an idiot. You're so full of your own arrogance and self-righteousness. I don't care how 'right' you are, your anger and arrogance and cruelty make you completely wrong. So why don't we just pop your pious bubble and let you sink to earth as the broken, flawed, and needy human being you are. Let's just have a good laugh at your idiocy. And from that basis, why don't you reach out to others with love, compassion, and creativity?"

So I prayed and reread Billy's original message. To my utter amazement, I agreed with almost every one of his points. His longtime New York style just rubbed me the wrong way. So rather than send another e-mail, I sought him out after a worship service, put my arm around him, and said, "Hey, your e-mail really ticked me off, Billy . . . but then I reread it and actually discovered that you were right on target. So let's get together and talk about it." Dropping our protective walls of self-righteousness always leads us deeper into loving Christian community.

The Kurnai people of Australia retell a myth about the need to release our bubble of pride and embrace community. According to their story, a fat frog named Dak swallowed the entire supply of earth's water. Try as they might, the thirsty animals couldn't force Dak to spit out the life-giving water. Grimly, tenaciously, humorlessly, Dak held the water in his big, fat mouth. Finally, a clever snake approached Dak and, twisting and contorting itself into ridiculous shapes, forced Dak to burst out laughing. The precious liquid was released, watering and refreshing the parched earth, bringing life in its trail.[9]

In the same way, as I continue to learn from the holy fools, especially the ultimate Holy Fool himself, God moves in and through my life. I take God seriously, but I laugh at myself. I'm open to the liberating truth about myself. The water of life flows among us. And as another practical result, I no longer hold ragged people at bay. Like Jesus and all the holy fools, I want to move toward them in love. Stripped of smugness, I'm ready for the next phase in the journey of holy folly: demolishing ghetto walls.

QUESTIONS FOR REFLECTION

Who has been your court jester or holy fool—the person who can speak truth into your life without fear of the consequences?

Where does the voracious "tapeworm" of self-righteousness appear in your system? Read the story of the older brother in Luke 15:25-32. How do you see yourself in his attitudes and behavior (consider the four symptoms of self-righteousness on pages 26–27)?

Helmut Thielicke wrote, "There are no festivals in this life, but only the tedious, tiresome, though highly serious monotony. . . . There is a kind of obedience that has about it a mildewed, numbing lack of freshness and vitality that never makes a person really happy." In what sense does this describe followers of Christ today? In what sense does it describe your life?

Do you consider yourself a defensive person? How do you respond to criticism? What would it mean to take yourself less seriously?

CHAPTER 3

Demolishing Ghetto Walls

Such is the axiom that the fool lives out: no healing without
solidarity, no salvation without participation.

KALLISTOS WARE

SIX YEARS AGO I READ the following headline in our small-town Minnesota newspaper: "Cambridge man pleads guilty to murder in fatal crash." Apparently "Lou Nelson," a short-time resident of our community, loaded up on alcohol, hopped into his 1989 Nissan Sentra, raced through the streets of northeast Minneapolis (eluding police officers along the way), sped straight through a stop sign, and slammed into another car, instantly killing the two cousins in that car. Based on prior offenses, Lou was sentenced by the court to nearly twenty years in jail.

Three months before the accident, Lou sat in my study at church and asked me to help him find God. I didn't like Lou at first. I thought he only wanted cash or food vouchers. With long, greasy hair, tobacco-stained teeth, arms covered with tattoos, and hauntingly sad and lonely eyes, Lou looked to me every bit the con artist. But Lou never asked for cash. He was driven by deeper hungers—staying out of jail, achieving sobriety and serenity, and finding his "higher power." Like the Prodigal Son, Lou was weary of eating pig slop and yearned to come home.

I never even considered inviting him to church. Lou was just too different—too ragged, too messy, too tattooed. I was pastoring an entire tribe of Lucky Tiger people—nice, respectable people with clean hair, white teeth, and untattooed arms. Unlike Lou, we were a tidy tribe who planned worship services and lots of other activities for nice families. A ragged guy like Lou would never fit into our culture of pristine spirituality. So I never tried to make him fit with us.

But after I read the headline about Lou's conviction, I was stunned by the gap between Lou's ragged state and our "tidy" state. It suddenly struck me that, for better or worse, I was dwelling in a Christian ghetto. Sociology 101 taught me that ghettos usually form when a minority group feels that it must band together and build walls around itself. A ghetto stems from basic natural needs for a sense of community survival and identity. Every group or organization needs boundary markers. These markers serve as fences to neatly divide the world into "innies" and "outies." They provide innies with security, comfort, and a sense of belonging. They also tell us who to exclude. Based on our boundary markers, Lou was clearly out. He lived in his ghetto; we lived in ours. *Vive la différence!*

And as far as most of us are concerned, everyone seems happy with the ghetto walls . . . except those disruptive and subversive holy fools I keep bumping into.

The Subversion of the Holy Fools

As I read the stories of the holy fools, I saw that they faced the same problem of the Christian ghetto, and it repulsed them. So they rebelled. Like someone trapped in a garage, desperate to avoid being slowly asphyxiated, they tore and clawed their way out of their Christian ghetto. They demolished the walls that separated them from outies by making contact with them, embracing them, and eventually wooing these prodigals back to the Father's house. Rather than waiting for ragged people to make the journey into the Christian ghetto, coaxing them over *our* fences, the holy fools actively sought and befriended people outside the ghetto walls.

As I started to collect stories of the holy fools, I noticed that throughout the church's history they insisted—loudly and dramatically—on the need to bust ghetto walls and identify with ragged sinners. I've already mentioned Symeon, the scandalous holy fool who, according to good church people, wasted far too much time on prostitutes, winos, and demoniacs. The holy fool Patrick spent most of his life in Ireland, loving and sharing the gospel with the ruthless people who had kidnapped him as a teenager. While walking along a road, Saint Francis of Assisi overcame his revulsion to physical ugliness and kissed the putrid face of a leper. "When I was in sin," Francis wrote, "the sight of lepers nauseated me beyond measure . . . [but] what had previously nauseated me became a source of spiritual and physical consolation for me." John Wesley, a proper and dignified English gentleman from the 1700s, considered it "almost a sin" to preach the gospel anywhere outside of a church building. But in order to identify with sinners, Wesley declared that he "submitted to be more vile" and preached in a brickyard near Bristol. From then on Wesley's "vile" ministry blossomed outdoors. Of the five hundred sermons he delivered from April to December 1739, only eight were in church buildings.

My favorite ghetto-busting story involves a man named Joseph de Veuster, also known as Damien the Leper. Joseph (or Damien) was born into a Belgian farming family and then studied for the ministry and moved to the Hawaiian Islands, where he started serving at a comfortable church. About the same time, the Hawaiian Islands were experiencing an outbreak of leprosy. The government took aggressive action by quarantining the lepers on the island of Molokai. The rugged beauty of Molokai became known for its sorrow and isolation. Between 1866 and 1873, nearly one thousand lepers arrived at Molokai, permanently cut off from family and friends, desperately poor, preparing to die from leprosy.

In 1873, at his own request, Damien moved to Molokai to pastor the lepers. His first house was the shade of a pandanus tree; his dining room table was a large rock. His supervisors told him to never touch a leper—which he gladly obeyed. The mangled faces and disfigured limbs, not to mention the putrid smell of rotting flesh, repulsed him. But soon Damien started touching and hugging the people, always addressing them as "my fellow lepers." Over the next eleven years, Damien taught the lepers to farm, build houses, play instruments, and even form a worship band. The lepers actually began to live fulfilled and happy lives. Then in December of 1884, while soaking his feet in hot water, Damien noticed that he couldn't feel the water. After eleven years Damien had become a leper—the final, dramatic stage of his identification with his "fellow lepers."

I also considered two contemporary holy fools named Leon and Nancy Finifrock. After raising their own children and working in separate careers, Leon and Nancy sensed a mutual call from God to open their home to a particular group of ragged sinners—adolescent foster boys. Over the past fifteen years, Leon and Nancy have welcomed nearly one hundred boys into their home in northeastern Minnesota. The state usually sends the boys to Leon and Nancy as a last resort; in most cases, nobody else wants them. The boys are the potato peelings of our societal dysfunction. But Leon and Nancy embrace them, demonstrating unconditional love, eating meals together, providing structure and discipline. They see it as a subversive and Jesus-like activity—breaking down ghetto walls and embracing ragged sinners for Jesus' sake.

Jesus, the Friend of Sinners

Naturally, leaving the ghetto and befriending ragged people can shock and scandalize those who are safely nestled inside the ghetto walls, but the holy fools found a powerful ally in Jesus, the friend of sinners. Of course, Jesus issued a clarion call to repentance, discipleship, and spiritual transformation. Jesus said and did things that were deemed strange and offensive, like dying on a cross (see 1 Corinthians 1:18-25). Nevertheless, sinners liked Jesus. They enjoyed his company and felt at ease in his presence. No serious New Testament scholar I've heard of has suggested this possibility, but I'm convinced that when Jesus was growing up, all the neighborhood kids knocked on Joseph and Mary's door and pleaded, "Can Jesus come out and play with us?" Based on Jesus' frequent dinner parties with sinners, it's not a shabby theory.

We do know that Jesus and sinners continually connected in

43

social settings. By befriending sinners, by moving with ease and even laughter in their presence (unless you think that those dinner parties were just one long-winded sermon), Jesus did more than just practice "friendship evangelism." He subverted the entire structure of the religious establishment by changing the boundary markers. He picked up the ghetto wall and moved it a few hundred miles down the street. In the process, he blew away our often rigid social categories of innies and outies—and he created a scandal.

For instance, when Jesus spotted a sawed-off runt named Zacchaeus, an unpopular chief tax collector and a clear outie who lived beyond the ghetto walls, Jesus invited himself over for dinner. By inviting himself for dinner, Jesus stirred up a chorus of boos and murmurs. And then after polishing off his meal, Jesus made the declaration, "Salvation has come to this home today, for this man has shown himself to be a true son of Abraham." In doing so, Jesus actively rearranged the fence posts (see Luke 19:1-10). "I want this outsider to belong," Jesus was in essence boldly declaring.

On another occasion, when Jesus told a story about a "Good" Samaritan (about as oxymoronic to them as a "good" terrorist would be to us), he wasn't just telling us to stop and loosen a few lug nuts on a stranger's flat tire (see Luke 10:30-37). He was challenging the most basic assumptions of the religious community of his day: Where does the ghetto wall end? Who's in? Who's out? Everyone drew careful lines to define who could not belong to their group; Jesus redrew the lines to embrace outcasts, sinners, demoniacs, the poor, and even his worst enemies and persecutors. "Listen," Jesus was basically saying. "My Father has invited even despised tax collectors and Samaritans—not to mention the prostitutes, the poor, the hungry, the thirsty, and the persecuted—to dine at his banquet of grace. Let's compel them to come to the great banquet" (see Luke 14:15-24).

So for Jesus and the holy fools, a deeply spiritual life flows naturally and easily into a life of solidarity with sinners. That's not to say it doesn't take hard work and intentionality. The holy fools' approach to holy living and spiritual disciplines didn't remove them from undesirable or "unholy" people; instead, they intentionally sought these people out, meeting them on their turf. That's why Symeon united with the despised and unloved dregs of his world, calling them "my brethren and companions." Merely preaching at or even conveying information isn't enough. Like Jesus, the holy fools refused to offer advice and "love" from a secure distance, merely lobbing it over the ghetto walls. No, they chose instead to leave the ghetto in order to "seek and save those who are lost" (Luke 19:10).

Commenting on the aim of the yurodivi in Russian society, Iulia de Beausobre said, "How does the [holy fool] pity, then, strive to mend the ill, to heal the wound, to bridge the gap? . . . It can only be done from man to man; by no amount of organizations or subscriptions, but only through a complete identification of oneself. He who pities another must leave his own place among the good people on the sunny side of the gap, must go out and find the other where he is; if he returns at all, it is with the other at his pace."[1] Or as Kallistos Ware said, holy fools were guided by a simple rule of life: "*No healing without solidarity, no salvation without participation.*"[2] We simply must leave the safety of our pristine ghettoes on the "sunny side of the gap" and join others on the dark side of the gap.

Is Solidarity Possible?

Of course, the huge difference between the original holy fools and present-day Christians is that they actually pulled it off. By and large, I wasn't standing in solidarity with those who dwelled outside our walls. I was too busy running a church, a tribe of neat, clean, churchy people. We'd wring our hands about this problem, but most of us didn't want to make personal contact with ragged sinners.

Christian community at its best will always glow with the radiance of Christ. But a Christian ghetto traps and isolates us, keeping us padlocked behind our huge iron gates—or, if we do break out of the ghetto, we often do more damage than good. We leave carnage in our wake when we act stiff and artificial and fail to pursue genuine relationships with real give-and-take, sincere listening, and admission of our mistakes. Unfortunately, there are days when the walls seem so concrete that I wonder if contemporary Western institutionalized Christianity can ever reach beyond its own ghetto existence. "What would it take," ponders Philip Yancey, "for a church to become a place where prostitutes, tax collectors, and even guilt-tinged Pharisees would gladly gather?"[3] I agonize over that question. What will it take for the church to become a haven for weary and ragged people?

I'm not supposed to say this or even think this, but there are really bad days when I answer Yancey's question with two words: Level everything. Level the present church with all its ghetto-shaping structures, traditions, organizations, and rules, and start from scratch. Just raze everything—fire the pastors, demolish the church buildings, disband the small groups, dismantle the committees—and then pray and worship for six months before starting over with Yancey's question burning in our hearts.

A Jesus-Like Approach

Fortunately, Jesus and most of the holy fools exhibited more patience than I do. And once again, the holy fools stood by to

mentor me in the fine art of spiritual subversion, this time showing me how to break down ghetto walls wisely. How did they
maintain a deep center in Christ and at the same time embrace
ragged people on a ragged journey to God? I could summarize
my observations about holy fools with three ghetto-busting,
Christlike practices: radical acceptance, radical pursuit, and radical hospitality.

The Practice of Radical Acceptance

First, the holy fools displayed a radical and shocking level of
acceptance toward ragged people on a ragged path to God. It's
certainly counterintuitive, but those early desert Christians, who
lived as heroic athletes for God, at the same time refused to judge
others who hadn't achieved their level of rigorous discipline when
it came to solitude, self-denial, and Scripture meditation. When
asked how he could live a holy life, one of the desert fathers told
his protégé: "Say at every moment, 'Who am I?' and then judge
no one." This radically nonjudgmental spirit became a hallmark
of desert spirituality.

A young man in one of the fourth-century desert communities fell into sin, and the other brothers expelled him from
their midst. Abba Antony (one of the trailblazers of the monastic
movement) took him in, restored him, and sent him back to the
community, but they rejected him again. Antony delivered the
following message: "A ship was wrecked in the ocean and lost
its cargo, and with great difficulty the empty ship was brought
to land. Now do you want to run the ship that has been res-
cued onto the rocks and sink it?" The brothers got the point and
accepted the sinful man at once.

On another occasion when a brother fell into sin, the leaders of the community invited the great Abba Moses to a special

disciplinary meeting. Moses refused to come, but after they insisted, he finally arrived with a huge basket of sand strapped to his back. As he silently walked into the meeting, the sand leaked onto the ground behind him. Finally he spoke: "My sins run out behind me and I do not see them and I have come here today to judge another." The community repented and gave the sinful brother a taste of grace.

These stories led me back to a more familiar story of another ragged man on a ragged path toward Jesus: Saul. Saul didn't exactly qualify as "church leadership potential." Borrowing an image from the snorting of wild animals, the storyteller Luke paints Saul "uttering threats with every breath and . . . eager to kill the Lord's followers" (Acts 9:1). He was a wild bully and a religious jerk, but then Jesus met him on the road with blinding light and dismantled Saul's life. After this initial encounter with Jesus, Saul was a pitiful mess. Blind, disoriented, and scorched, he was taken by the hand and dropped off by his traveling companions somewhere in Damascus.

Through the love of two holy fools, two believers who practiced radical acceptance, Jesus reassembled Saul and transformed him from a persecutor of the faith into an apostle for the faith (see Acts 9). First, a man named Judas (and perhaps his wife) opened their home to Saul, the former ravager of the church (see Acts 7:58; 8:3). Second, God called a man named Ananias to come and pray for Saul. Initially, Ananias balked at God's lack of safety standards, but he eventually obeyed and found Saul. In a deeply moving gesture of acceptance, Ananias placed his hands on Saul, embracing him as "Brother Saul," and prayed for God's blessing to fall on Saul. Through the act of radical acceptance, Saul became God's "chosen instrument."

This was Christian community at its best: reluctant and frightened, but also daring in its outward-focused acceptance.

It's an antighetto, a community of radically accepting, nonjudging people.

The desert Christians could also be demanding in holding men and women to the high and holy calling of following Jesus in a corrupt culture. But as I listened to their stories, I was starting to find ways to practice radical acceptance myself. About three years ago a young graduate student came into our church family who brought this concept to life. She was brilliant and beautiful, but she had also been deeply wounded. After living with an abusive father and a neglectful mother for most of her life, she struggled to trust anyone—including God. She vacillated between faith and nonfaith, trusting Jesus wholeheartedly one day and then fleeing from him the next day. We never chastised her for her doubt and fear. Instead, a university professor from our church met with her and calmly talked with her about her intellectual questions about faith. An older woman met with her regularly to bake cookies. Our small group threw a birthday bash for her (the first real birthday party she'd ever had in her life). Through it all, we just kept loving her and embracing her. At one point she told me, "I don't know if I can handle this much love—it almost feels like it's burning my skin. I've never felt so scared and so sheltered and accepted at the same time. If I try to run away, please keep loving me." And in the footsteps of the holy fools, that's exactly what we did.

The Practice of Radical Pursuit

Jesus did more than just accept sinners; he actively pursued them. New Testament scholar Craig Keener comments, "Jewish literature indicates that, for all of Judaism's heavy emphasis on repentance and divine mercy, Jesus' act of *pursuing* sinners was unheard of."[4] Jesus himself defined his mission in terms of an active pursuit: "If a man has a hundred sheep and one of them gets lost, what will he do? Won't he leave the ninety-nine others in the wilderness and go to search for the one that is lost until he finds it?" (Luke 15:4).

Once again, I discovered that the desert holy fools were crazy enough to take Jesus seriously. In one deeply moving story, Abba Abraham, a desert father known for his great holiness, received word that his seven-year-old niece had become an orphan. Abraham gladly welcomed her to his desert hut, allowing her to stay in the outer room of his cell. As Mary matured, she became a young woman of great beauty. But one day while Abraham was on a short trek deeper in the desert, a wicked monk visited and, enraptured with Mary's beauty, raped her. Mary, tortured by guilt and despair, fled to a distant city, where she found a job in a brothel. Abraham returned from his short journey and looked everywhere for Mary. After searching for two years, he finally followed clues and located Mary in the distant city. In the spirit of Jesus, who set aside his glory to stand beside sinful people, Abraham put aside his monk's garb and, borrowing a military uniform and even a horse, fled the desert to pursue Mary in the city.

When he finally found the brothel, still disguised as a powerful soldier, Abraham demanded to see the "fine wench" named Mary. "I've come a long way for the love of Mary," he told the innkeeper. And then the desert ascetic, who had subsisted on bread and water for nearly forty years, devoured a chunk of red meat. After supper, Mary took the "officer" to her room. As she bent down to untie his shoes, her uncle quietly repeated, "Yes, I've come a long way for the love of Mary." Mary recognized her uncle's voice and fell at his feet, weeping. Because of his devotion to Jesus and "for the love of Mary," Abba Abraham fled the ghetto walls and pursued a ragged sinner. And if her uncle could pursue a ragged person like Mary, how much more could Mary expect from the God who is "rich in mercy" (Ephesians 2:4)?[5]

How do we actively pursue people outside our ghetto walls? My friend Denis Haack reminded me that programs and committees don't pursue "sinners"; only people leave ghetto walls and make contact with those far from God. And usually the people who make contact are the ones who engage in simple but subversive acts—like actually showing interest in people's lives, asking good questions, and listening. Haack claims that the art of listening is one of the "most radical expressions of Christian faithfulness possible in our postmodern world." Unfortunately, it's "so rare in evangelical circles as to constitute a scandalous denial of the Gospel."[6]

I can't identify a more powerful way to demonstrate the radical pursuit of Jesus than setting aside my agenda, tuning in to another heart, and actually listening. A few months ago, after dropping my son off an hour early for his soccer game, I stretched out in my car with a new copy of a Pulitzer Prize–winning novel. Ah, the sweetness of a new book on a Saturday afternoon in spring. As I cranked back my seat and opened to page 1, a fellow soccer dad knocked on my car window.

"Hey, what are you doing right now?" he asked.

"Well, Joe, I'm trying to read this new book here."

He didn't pick up my nonverbal clues. "Hey, can I tell you something?"

"Sure, go ahead, Joe."

"My cousin just died this week—it's the fourth funeral in the past six months."

I cranked up the seat and said, "Wow, that is tough. I'm so sorry to hear that."

Joe said, "Do you want to go for a ride?"

"Sure, I'll go for a ride with you." So for an hour we drove around Long Island, and I listened to the ache and fear in his heart. Jesus is pursuing Joe. As a follower of Jesus, I am committed to pursuing others too. As I continue to follow Jesus and as I'm available to others, Jesus will lead me deeper into the pursuit of sought-after people like Joe. Like Abba Abraham, I'm called to a life of sacrifice and risk as I share the Good News of Jesus with others.

Eventually, we'll talk about Jesus. He knows that I know Jesus, but I want to tell him why that matters so much. I'll do that soon. But for now I'm trying to heed what my friend Denis said about pursuing people by listening to them. "Can you think of a more meaningful expression of love? If you can't remember such a time, doesn't your heart ache for it?" Based on the example of the holy fools, I am learning that pursuit is perhaps the most powerful "program" or "strategy" of demolishing ghetto walls.

The Practice of Radical Hospitality

Every culture realizes that something special happens when people sit down and eat together. So we develop rules and rituals and even taboos about what we eat, when we eat, and whom we eat with. In the Old Testament and in the culture of Jesus' day, eating contained profound symbolic meaning. Eating with someone signified acceptance, approval, welcome, and intimacy. More than that, one's "culinary theology"—which foods are acceptable to eat, what rituals are required for food preparation, and what people could sit at your dinner table—established clear boundary markers, those highly visible practices that define innies and outies. Meals were social statements. When people gathered for a little lunch, the stakes were enormously high. Eating with the wrong people could mean exclusion from the worshiping community for months.

Jesus knew exactly what he was doing when he ate with sinners. He was making a statement—not only rewriting the rules about hospitality but also casting a new vision for the Kingdom of God. By eating with sinners and drawing the ire of those who thought he should know better (see Matthew 9:9-13 and Luke 15:1-2 for a few examples), Jesus declared the nature of God's reign. In Jesus, God broke down the walls between a holy God and a sinful humanity.

And then Jesus told us to follow his example. Jesus had a secret strategy for standing in solidarity with people outside our ghetto walls. Are you ready to hear it? It's a revolutionary approach. It's gutsy, bold, and daring. Here it is: Throw parties, but revise your guest list first. That's the plan. I told you it was daring. While Jesus was attending a dinner party (see Luke 14:1-14), he gave his host some advice: "When you put on a luncheon or a banquet . . . don't invite[7] your friends, brothers, relatives, and rich neighbors." What's the problem with habitually inviting people inside the ghetto walls? They'll pay you back, Jesus said. What's wrong with that? Jesus didn't say, but I imagine it reinforces our self-centered ghetto mentality that life is about me and the little tribe of people I prefer to associate with. Jesus was constantly pushing out the ghetto walls (see also Luke 6:32-36).

Jesus told his host that instead of just inviting friends within the ghetto walls, he should invite four categories of people: the poor, the crippled, the lame, and the blind. Once again, Jesus was making a statement. Everyone knew that a particular religious community[8] in Jesus' day had specifically declared that the poor, the crippled, the lame, and the blind didn't belong inside their ghetto walls. By urging his host to target and invite those four groups of people, Jesus was subverting one aspect of the religious establishment. And, Jesus warned, they may not pay you back. They may not be grateful. They may have bad manners and foul language. You may lose your favorite seat at the table. These ragged outsiders may interfere with your ghetto conversations. But, Jesus promised, "God will reward you." In other words, if you really believe in heaven, then it will affect whom you eat with in this life. If you really believe in the "resurrection of the righteous," your dinner table will include lost people. Throw parties and revise your guest list.

As far as I know, no one practices this simple strategy better than my wife. She's enough of a holy fool to actually throw a party and revise her guest list. Before our first anniversary Julie informed me that she was planning a "little party" for all the people we knew. I figured our tiny bungalow living room could accommodate about twenty people. I had no idea that Julie would literally go into the highways and byways and compel people to come in (see Luke 14:23). Nearly eighty people swarmed into our living room: Sudhar, a Sikh with a huge turban; Simone from Nigeria; Brad, a drug addict; Mark, an uptight present-day Pharisee—a motley crew of lost and saved mingling, eating, and laughing together. We didn't have an altar call, but we did invoke the presence of the risen Christ into our midst. For a moment in time, the ghetto walls came down, and Jesus walked in our midst.

I can't help but think of the desert fathers and mothers here. In our context it's easy to assume they were avoiding hospitality by living lives of solitude in the middle of nowhere. But in a strange way, by moving to the desert, they actually had *more* of an impact on those around them, not less. People heard about their holiness and sought them out. Their lives were so attractive, so courageous and uncontrolled by the forces around them that others wanted to know the secret to their spiritual freedom in Christ. And most challenging to me, the desert fathers emphasized the rule of hospitality over the rule of spiritual rigor. In other words, if abbas or ammas in the desert were fasting or practicing solitude, they would often (not always, but often) forgo their spiritual practices in order to display hospitality for their guest. In short, hospitality trumped asceticism.[9]

Embracing Ragged Sinners

Someone may object that my Jesus-based strategy doesn't exactly qualify for evangelism. In the sense that I haven't outlined a method to verbally proclaim the content of the gospel to those who don't know Christ, I would agree with that assessment. But then again, I'm arguing that Jesus made contact first and then presented the content of the gospel. I'm afraid that we've become so ghettoized that we no longer make contact with "sinners"— and we like it that way.

Again, the holy fools startle and shock us. *My God*, we wake up and pray, *have I really lived behind these walls for so long? Jesus, forgive me. Move me out of here. Let us dismantle the walls and join you in seeking and saving the lost.* We remember the motto for holy fools from every age: "There is no healing without solidarity, no salvation without participation."

So to return to Philip Yancey's question: "What would it take for a church to become a place where prostitutes, tax collectors, and even guilt-tinged Pharisees would gladly gather?" I would answer: It takes holy folly—and not just one or two holy fools but an entire community of holy fools. If it takes a village to raise a child, it also certainly takes a community to embrace fellow sinners and raise new followers of Jesus.

About a year ago a bunch of big, tough-looking, pasta-addicted Italian guys with names like Sal and Vinny and Johnny rented the abandoned restaurant next to our church building. They were trying to create a fine dining experience in an ugly part of town. Even after everyone told them it was a dumb idea (in five years this location had chewed up five restaurants), they did it anyway. They called it "316" because it was located at 316 Main Street.

As they were getting ready to open for business, I paid a visit because (1) I'm a very nice Christian neighbor and (2) I wanted to scope out the building so that after the restaurant failed we could use it for a cool young adult worship service. But when Sal and Vinny and Johnny discovered I was a local pastor, they asked me to come back in a week and bless the building. Of course this put me in a tough spot: How do you bless something you want to fail?

A week later I returned and offered one of the most insincere blessings ever given in two thousand years of professional Christian blessings. It was very awkward. They kept calling me "Father," and I kept waiting for the Godfather to show up. They begged me to stay for a drink, so when I asked for ginger ale, they laughed hysterically and poured me a glass of their best Scotch. (Just for the record, I hate Scotch, but I did sip some of it before that night's elder meeting.) My wife and I became good buddies with Sal and Johnny and Vinny. They let us eat expensive meals at 316 for free. When my wife read to them 3:16 from the Gospel of John, they were so moved they framed it and hung it in the middle of the restaurant. I even repented and started praying with utter sincerity that God would bless 316. We invited them to church, and Johnny actually showed up for Easter Sunday and occasional Sundays after that. Another guy named Guido or Jimmy wanted to come, but Vinny told me he had to spend a few years at "college" (i.e., the local jail).

About two months later, Johnny pulled me aside after a worship service. He showed me a pretty little box and said, "I want you to pray for this box." After praying for a building, I figured I could pray for a box. "Sure, Johnny, but what's in there?" Tears welled up in his eyes as he said, "These are the ashes of my twenty-nine-year-old daughter. She was murdered in Las Vegas. She told me that she had found Jesus through a church out there, but then she was shot. Will you bless her remains, and will your church help me do a memorial service for her?" My heart shattered, I gasped for air, and I whispered, "Of course we'll be there for you, Johnny." I couldn't meet Johnny's request to pray for dead remains, but I would do everything in my power to walk beside Johnny in the depths of his grief.

The next week my wife and some other folks from the church helped me with the memorial service. We packed out the place with big Italian guys who stood by Johnny and wept like babies. I spoke from Isaiah 53 about how we're all just a bunch of lost sheep but Jesus loves us like a Good Shepherd. They wept even louder. Through it all, I was proud of our church family. I had started out acting like a religious jerk, but God used the entire church anyway to reach beyond our ghetto walls. We were acting like a whole community of holy fools.

How do we heal the wounds of broken people living in a broken world? It doesn't happen with programs or strategies. It happens person to person, through a complete identification of oneself with others. And it happens not just with a solo holy fool but with an entire community committed to a lifestyle of holy folly.

QUESTIONS FOR REFLECTION

How high are the ghetto walls in your life, your family, your small group, or your church? Which groups of people would not feel welcome? Is there anything you can do to change that?

Reread the story of Jesus' encounter with Zacchaeus in Luke 19:1-10. How did Jesus reach over the ghetto walls and embrace Zacchaeus?

How do we practice radical acceptance and yet at the same time avoid condoning sin?

Can you think of someone in your life Jesus seems to be pursuing? Pray for that person right now and then ask yourself, *What else can I do to practice a Christlike pursuit of my friend?*

What would it take for you to practice one part of Jesus' simple strategy for evangelism—to throw a party but revise your guest list? Who would you invite? Go ahead, revise your guest list. When could you throw this party, and who could help you with it?

AWAKENING TO A LIFE
OF VULNERABILITY

CHAPTER 4

Receiving the Gift of Tears

In every age, and above all in this present deeply uneasy,
tired and restless age, nothing is more essential than
repentance.

SERAPHIM PAPAKOSTAS

SHORTLY AFTER MY FORTY-SEVENTH BIRTHDAY, my dad handed me
a thick manila envelope containing all my report cards from kindergarten through college. Looking over the stack of cards, the
memories came flooding back—even from kindergarten. Ah,
sweet kindergarten, the best and worst year of my life. The agony
of separation anxiety. The wrinkled but kind face of my teacher,
the thirty-year veteran Mrs. Floaten. The challenge of stacking

bright yellow blocks with my new friend Kevin. The stress of "practicing good health habits" (my highest grade) and "taking part in conversations" (my lowest grade). Kindergarten served as my fiery purgatory, tossing me into the flames of social maturation, as well as "good safety habits" and "creative activities."

And yet, in spite of all its benefits, I'm glad it's over. I have no regrets; I had to pass through it. But I also have no interest in repeating it. Ah, kindergarten, my inferno and my first love, the brightest and darkest year of my life; I'm happy I'll never pass through your doors again.

In the spiritual realm, kindergarten is a lot like repentance: It's an important stage of development and it changes us profoundly, but we certainly don't want to repeat it. At least that's the way I viewed repentance before I met the holy fools. As they mentored me on the spiritual path, God sent me back to spiritual kindergarten—and I resented the demotion. I had done my time in the halls of repentance more than thirty years ago. I definitely knew some people who needed a refresher course from spiritual kindergarten, but I was moving into spiritual PhD studies.

Who needs to repeat the kindergarten of repentance over and over again? Everyone, said the holy fools. The holy fools placed repentance at the center of their spirituality. They called it *penthos,* or compunction—a medical term for puncturing or piercing with a scalpel.[1] When we confront simple reality, claimed the holy fools, when God flips on the light switch in our lives, our hearts are pierced by the scalpel of God's truth. Like the prophet Isaiah, we encounter the holiness of God and we are "undone" (see Isaiah 6:1-6, KJV). Like the apostle Peter after he denied Jesus three times, we remember the face of Christ and weep (see Mark 14:72). Like the crowds who first heard the Good News about a crucified and risen Savior, we, too, are cut to the heart by our distance from and our longing for God (see Acts 2:37).

And in contrast to my former spiritual practices, the holy fools claimed that this process never ends. God pierces the heart again and again. As I continued to meet holy fools, I noticed that they viewed repentance as the essential curriculum for spiritual kindergarten, college, and postdoctoral studies. In other words, we never "graduate" out of repentance. We begin the spiritual journey with repentance, and every step we take follows with a deep, continuing sense of repentance. While he was lying on his deathbed, the disciples of the holy fool and desert father Sisoes assured him that he had finally ended the journey of repentance. "Truly," the holy old man replied, "I am not sure whether I have even begun to repent." For the holy fools, repentance continues until our last breath.

I was starting to understand. In those sacred halls of repentance, God was splitting me wide open. For the first time in years, I wept, the hot tears streaming down my face, soaking the open Bible I often held on my lap. What else could I do? God had pierced my heart with the clean knife of repentance, and I was undone.

A Tearful Soul

I didn't know it at the time, but according to the holy fools these hot tears of repentance were actually a sign of God's grace. They called them "the gift of tears." For many holy fools, the experience of compunction, the piercing of the heart, was so intense that it often produced a stream of literal tears. As the holy fools continued to mentor me, I discovered that the tears of repentance flow when God strikes the dirt of our hearts, piercing our sin-hardened lives with his blade, loosening the packed earth of our lives, and digging up the soil, until finally, when the gentle rains fall, the seeds of new life sprout and grow.

I encountered numerous stories of holy fools who received

this gift of tears. According to one story I read from the desert Christians, the godly Arsenius wore a cloth around his neck so he could wipe the tears that continually streamed from his eyes. Wherever he went, working in the field or praying in his cell, God softened and broke Arsenius's heart until the tears of sorrow and love flowed from his eyes. A few years later I read about the desert Christian John Climacus urging fellow believers to prayerfully guard the gift of tears. "When the soul grows tearful, weeps, and is filled with tenderness," he wrote, "and all this without having striven for it, then let us run, for the Lord has arrived uninvited. . . . Guard those tears like the apple of your eye until they go away."[2]

After his profound encounter with Christ,[3] Francis entered into a deeper time of repentance, climbing Mount Subasio, passing through the black firs to hide in a cave. Away from the noise of the city and the chaos of his past life, Francis wept. With a flood of tears, Francis reviewed his past life of self-indulgence, and it broke his heart. God struck him with the enormity of his sin. Over the next few months, Francis returned to his secret hideout often.[4]

For the holy fools, penthos and the gift of tears provided the only sure path to growth in Christ. When one of the desert believers asked his mentor how to deal with the sin in his life, the old man replied, "Weep, for there is no other way." A disordered, hardened heart refuses to crack. But a heart touched by God's grace breaks wide open until the tears of repentance gently flow. Repent, weep, soften your heart, for there is no other way.

Just a Scary God Word?

Again I met the subversion of the holy fools, and at least initially, it disturbed me. "Weep, for there is no other way." Isn't that just a wee bit negative? Who wants to spend his life weeping into a handkerchief that is permanently attached to his chest? What kind of worm theology is that? What's the point of all this groveling and psychological self-flagellation? I'm not surprised that contemporary author and poet Kathleen Norris placed *repent* on her list of "scary" Christian words that "bombarded" her and seemed "dauntingly abstract" and "even vaguely threatening."[5] Personally, I just wanted to master five principles for successful Christian living and get on with my life. All this talk about weeping and repenting was threatening my self-esteem.

Was this picture of repentance extreme? Well, perhaps, but once again, it was a rude and disruptive but utterly Spirit-inspired wake-up call for my sluggish soul. I need the extreme perspective from the holy fools. It doesn't require much social research to observe that we're still sinning; we just shift the blame. Repentance isn't hip anymore; instead, we've created a penthos-lite culture.

My fellow Minnesotan Garrison Keillor wrote a hilarious essay called "The Current Crisis in Remorse." It's written by a fictitious social worker who was once employed as a "professional remorse officer" in the Department of Human Services. The poor guy didn't even get an office—just a desk across from the elevator and a phone that he had to share with the director of the Nephew Program in Family Counseling. "Morale in remorse has never been lower," he complains. "We in remorse are a radical minority within the social-work community. We believe that not every wrong in our society is the result of complex factors such as poor early-learning environment and resultative dissocialized communication. Some wrong is the result of badness. We believe that some people act like jerks. . . . They do bad things. They should feel sorry for what they did and stop it."[6]

Apparently it takes a humorist to issue a prophetic call to compunction. Sadly, I've spent a good chunk of my Christian life becoming so "spiritually mature" that I think I've grown beyond the need for repentance. Of course, this makes me just like Jesus' first band of followers. You may recall that when Jesus interrupted dinner and mentioned that one of them would betray him, they all howled in protest, "Surely not I, Lord?" (Matthew 26:22, NIV). That's the same cry uttered through the ages in every sour marriage, every conflicted church, every relational breakdown, every hard-core addict: Surely, not I, Lord! But there's an ironic twist to the gospel story: By the time Jesus was nailed to a cross, every single disciple had betrayed Jesus on some level. Judas betrayed Jesus with his greed, and eventually each of the other disciples betrayed Jesus out of weakness, laziness, fear, or cowardice (see Mark 14:27-72).

As I continue to meet and read the stories of holy fools, the gift of tears is starting to make more sense. To them there was nothing unnatural or neurotic about repentance or the gift of tears. Actually, the flow of tears was the most natural thing in the world. They never conjured up repentance by asking, "Hmm, let's see, how can I feel lousy and beat myself up today?" The holy fools asked a much different question: "How can I stay awake and alert in God's presence?" Then they simply stood in God's presence, listening to his Word and daring enough to pray (and really mean it), "Search me, O God, and know my heart" (Psalm 139:23). When God answers that prayer, the tears flow. To stand in God's presence, completely unmasked, and pay attention to reality—the reality of our coldness and distance from God, the reality of his grace, the reality of the world's deep brokenness and our indifference to it—is enough to break our hearts and cause the tears to flow.

For the holy fools this "compunction of sorrow," as they called it, was only half of repentance. The other half consisted of the "compunction of desire." In other words, when we see the beauty of God—his holiness and love—we are filled with a deep yearning for God to come near. In her beautiful and simple book called *The Way of Repentance*, Irma Zaleski captures both the heartbreaking sorrow and heart-igniting desire of compunction:

> We repent because, when we catch even the tiniest glimpse of God, of his perfection and beauty, we are filled with longing and love. At the same time, our hearts break with sadness, because we realize how far we are from this perfection and beauty, how far our world is from it. . . . And above all, our hearts break because we realize that the source of this separation does not lie somewhere outside ourselves, but in our hearts themselves; the chains that bind us are the chains of our own self-centeredness.[7]

Both the compunction of sorrow and the compunction of desire combine to crack our hearts wide open. Sadly, we often drag ourselves through life half-asleep, overcome by the drudgery of the world. "I am surrounded by the corpses of souls," laments Father Smith in Walker Percy's novel *Love in the Ruins*. But like a jolt of electricity coursing through our bodies, compunction shocks and stings, penetrating our souls and awakening us to the wonder and beauty of God. Compunction sets our feet on a journey, and although we see how far we have to go, we long to continue the journey. The point of repentance isn't just to make us feel bad; it infuses us with hope and desire, specifically the hope and desire that God can change us, that God's mercy is available to us, that every breath we take is a gift from a merciful God.

As I reenter the school of repentance, the sorrow comes first—tears of sadness and regret. God plunges a dagger into my heart. It is the only way to wake me up. But then the sadness turns to desire. I yearn to know God better. One of the desert holy fools reprimanded a brash young protégé by telling him, "You think you're so far on the journey of life, but you're really just like a man who hasn't even found the right ship let alone put your baggage aboard and started the journey across the sea. And yet you talk like you've already arrived." Now I'm beginning to see that I am the brash young man. My journey is just beginning. But in true repentance the sorrow quickly gives way to a holy desire for God. With a renewed intensity, I want to pack my bags, board the ship, and set sail. I want to journey closer to God and others—and I don't care who I impress or how ragged I look. I just crave God.

The Opposite of Compunction

Much to my surprise, the holy fools taught me that the opposite of repentance isn't some kind of plastic happiness or a positive self-esteem; it's a hard heart. Like a big ugly rock, a hard heart never breaks, never gets punctured, and never weeps. It just stays hard, resisting and deflecting the waterfall of God's grace. No wonder the psalmist warned us, "Don't harden your hearts" (Psalm 95:8). When the writer Franz Kafka advised a friend about choosing good reading material, he said, "I think we ought to read only books that bite us and sting us. If the book we are reading doesn't shake us awake like a blow on the skull, why bother reading it in the first place. . . . A book must be the axe for the frozen sea within us."[8] Repentance is God's axe to break up the frozen sea in our hard hearts.

A hard heart can soften, but more often than not, God must pierce it and crack it open. During my return to the kindergarten of repentance, I reread a short story I had been introduced to twenty years earlier during college—Flannery O'Connor's

"Greenleaf." Like most of O'Connor's stories, "Greenleaf" brutally exposes our need for grace. The story opens by focusing on Mrs. Greenleaf, a large and eccentric woman who lives with her family on Mrs. May's farm. On a daily basis, Mrs. Greenleaf scours the newspapers for the day's most tragic and heartrending stories. With the clippings in hand, she treks into the woods, digs a hole, and buries the stories in the ground. Then, throwing her massive body on the dirt, she prays and shrieks over the hurt and pain, "Jesus, Jesus. Oh Jesus, stab me in the heart!" Mrs. Greenleaf knows the explosive power and strength of penthos. Her face is "as composed as a bulldog's." She prays like a desert warrior: loving but also plucky, fierce, and tenacious. As I reread the story, I realized that Mrs. Greenleaf is a classic holy fool.

In contrast, the landowner in the story, Mrs. May, considers herself a competent, proper, and decent Christian person—just like the Lucky Tiger people and me. The spectacle of her farm tenant writhing on the ground repulses her. "Jesus would be *ashamed* of you," she scolds Mrs. Greenleaf. Mrs. May possesses a stone-like heart that displays a self-righteous drive to control and dominate. Her obsession for control and power lead her to demand the slaughter of the Greenleafs' scrub bull just for the "exhilaration of carrying her point." One day, after she enrages the bull by honking her truck horn, the bull runs at her as she stands transfixed. In O'Connor's conclusion, before Mrs. May could react . . .

> The bull had buried his head in her lap, like a wild tormented lover. . . . One of the horns sank until it pierced her heart and the other curved around her side and held her in an unbreakable grip. She continued to stare straight ahead but the entire scene in front of her had changed . . . and she had the look of a person whose sight had been suddenly restored but who finds the light unbearable.[9]

As I reread the story, I finally grasped O'Connor's shock technique. The Holy Spirit wants to wake me up. Mrs. May, who all her life had stabbed others in the back with her "respectable" spirituality—her need to control and dominate—is stabbed, pierced, cut by the sword of God's grace. Spiritually speaking, I am often Mrs. May. The bull, like God himself, is powerful and "likes to bust loose." And like the bull's horns, God's grace is penetrating and holds me in its "unbreakable grip." At the end of the story, O'Connor shows us Mrs. May, gored by the bull's horns, bending over and "whispering some last discovery into the animal's ear." I realized that the raw goring is not a piercing of punishment; it is a piercing of love and mercy, an invitation to a transformed life. For in that violent piercing, Mrs. May suddenly encounters the wild Lover of her soul, the only one who could restore her sight and heal her soul.

The Surprising Joy of Repentance

Much to my surprise, the holy fools were never burdened by the gift of tears. Instead, they threw their arms wide open to receive the heart-piercing work of God and the tears that often accompanied it. These wacky holy fools had tasted the secret fruit of penthos: joy. Not just sorrow or fear or gut-wrenching honesty, but joy. Somehow they knew that when "the Lord has arrived uninvited," as John Climacus put it, cracking our hearts wide open, his grace gushes through the cracks.

For instance, when Jesus met that sawed-off runt named Zacchaeus, God split his heart wide open with penthos. It's certainly not a dreary story (see Luke 19:1-10). God's grace came pouring through the cracks. A fire started burning in the frosty corners of Zacchaeus's heart, awakening a holy desire to do justice and display compassion. True repentance, a compunction that pierces and transforms the human heart, always occurs in the context of God's lavish grace.

Unfortunately, throughout the history of Christian spirituality, many Christ followers (including some holy fools) exhibited a heavy, dreary, and utterly joyless approach to repentance. In her stimulating book entitled *Dancing in the Streets: A History of Collective Joy*, Barbara Ehrenreich contends that Jesus' followers abandoned his basically pro-joy approach to life. As an example, she mentions one hero of Protestant circles: John Bunyan. In her view, Bunyan's view of repentance and spirituality sucked every vestige of joy out of his heart. "John Bunyan seems to have been jolly enough in his youth," she contends, "much given to dancing and sports in the village green, but with the onset of his religious crisis these pleasures had to be put aside. Dancing was the hardest to relinquish . . . but he eventually managed to achieve a fun-free life. In *Pilgrim's Progress* the Bunyan-like hero Christian finds that any time he lets down his guard and experiences a moment of rest or even just diminished anxiety, he has lost ground or been sorely taken advantage of."[10]

In contrast to Bunyan's experience, Jesus clearly stated that penthos leads to joy. In Luke 15, for instance, on three occasions with three stories Jesus emphasized the sheer reckless, heart-thumping joy of God and his angels when Jesus seeks, finds, and softens even one hard heart. Wallowing in our shame and guilt isn't God's idea of repentance. Actually, for those who are in Christ, perpetual condemnation comes from Satan, not God (see Romans 8:1 and Revelation 12:10). The journey of repentance will be steep, but the view always leads to a summit drenched in joy. Psalm 30 puts it this way: "Weeping may last through the night, but joy comes with the morning" (verse 5); "You have turned my mourning into joyful dancing. You have taken away my clothes of mourning and clothed me with joy" (verse 11).

How to Let the Tears Flow

So how do we receive the gift of tears? How do I allow God to crack my heart open with true Christ-honoring compunction? First of all, for the holy fools, repentance wasn't a "work" to be performed that earns merit with God. None of our acts of contrition—tears, confessions, emotional agony—earn God's love and forgiveness. Christ has paid the debt and borne the shame of our sins. We don't add to God's grace and our forgiveness by our feelings or actions of repentance. Someone has stated it this way: The irreligious don't repent at all; the religious only repent of sins, but Christians also repent of their righteousness. Moral and religious people are sorry for their sins, but they see sins as simply the failure to live up to the standards by which they are saving themselves. They may go to Jesus for forgiveness—but only as a way to "cover over the gaps" in their project of self-salvation. But Christians are people who have adopted a whole new system of approaching God. They realize their entire reason for trying either to please God or to avoid God has been essentially the same—and essentially wrong! Christians realize that both their sins and their best deeds have all really been ways of avoiding Jesus as Savior.

"Irreligious people" attempt to construct their own sense of morality without reference to God or to Jesus Christ. "Religious people" believe in God and try hard to please him through religious practices and rituals and rules. So they may attend worship services, avoid sinful behaviors, join a local church, follow the church's rules and obligations, and try hard to become a "good" person. But just like the irreligious people, religious people end up avoiding God's path to acceptance and new life—through faith in Jesus Christ. Both groups avoid the Cross as the only solution to our problem of separation from a holy God.

The holy fools recognized that trying to achieve forgiveness on our own merit is futile. Based on their gospel-centered and grace-centered approach to the spiritual life, repentance is simply a matter of coming home and resting in Jesus. As the fourth-century pastor (and holy fool) John Chrysostom urged:

> Like the prodigal, let us also return home . . . no matter how far we have gotten carried away in our journey. Let us go back to our Father's house, not lingering over the length of the journey. For we shall find, if we be willing, that the way back again is very easy and very speedy. Only let us leave this strange land of sin where we have been drawn away from the Father. For our Father has a natural yearning toward us and will honor us if we are changed. He finds great pleasure in receiving back his children.[11]

Repentance means crying, "Abba, Father" and returning home. Thus, the holy fools would also remind us that we can't "crank up" tears or even an inner attitude of compunction. So don't agonize about the absence of tears. Nobody can produce tears at will. However, we can pray for a softened heart. "First pray for the gift of tears," urged the early desert father Evagrius, "to soften by compunction the inherent hardness of your soul."

A friend of mine recently told me about a time she had to ask God to soften her heart. A number of years ago her son played on a Little League baseball team coached by an angry, verbally abusive man. The coach never let the "scrubs" play—including her son, who showed up for every practice (remember, we're talking about thirteen-year-olds here). The coach would routinely scream at the kids and even cuss out his own son. According to my friend, this man seemed to project his dreams and frustrations onto his youngest son. By the end of the season, this frustrated mom was relieved to finally sever ties with this miserable man.

But a few years later she started running into him at church. The jerk even had the nerve to join the praise team! According to his story, God had changed his life, healing his rage and alcoholism and turning his life around for good. My friend couldn't believe it. She couldn't even look at him as he joyfully played his guitar. And she certainly did not want God to soften her heart. *Sorry, but God can't change people that fast,* she stewed. And every Sunday her attitudes of anger and resentment were thwarting her attempts to worship God.

Finally she chose to ask God to soften her heart—not for the coach's sake but for her own. Her prayer certainly didn't get answered overnight. But in the next few months my friend, who was struggling as a single mother of two sons, needed some major work done on her roof. She called six roofing companies, but they were either too busy or too expensive. Then, by more than mere coincidence, the former coach showed up with his roofing company. The roof was so dilapidated that it took him more days than expected, but he roofed the entire house for free. God had answered her reluctant prayer; he had softened her heart with the beauty of repentance.

We can also intentionally avoid the habits that continually harden us against God's heart-softening work: the sin of blaming, judging, and comparing ourselves with others. Early in his journey as a holy fool, Antony heard the voice of God say, "Turn your attention to yourself." Antony never used an internal focus to justify a lack of compassion. (Antony also stressed that "our life and our death is with our neighbor.") Rather, Antony and the holy fools stressed a nonjudgmental spirit. Nothing hardens my heart more than focusing on, obsessing over, and judging my neighbors for their faults and sins. But by paying attention to my own heart, I stay alert and aware of the ways God needs to change my heart.

Finally, confession is communal as well as private. Most of us are familiar with the personal, individual side of confession. But a penitent heart also grows and softens every time we're brutally honest about our sin *in the context of community.* "Confess your sins to each other," commanded the apostle James (James 5:16). He meant it; we view it as optional. Restoring the ancient practice of honestly sharing our sin with another human being keeps us in touch with the reality of our hearts. Our sin leads to secrecy; we want to run and hide. But the hiding only stiffens and hardens our heart. "Confession . . . hurts," wrote Dietrich Bonhoeffer, "it cuts a man down, it is a blow to pride."[12] But as we stand before a brother or sister in Christ, confessing our sin, our hearts will start to soften.

Communal confession doesn't imply that I confess my sins in front of two hundred or two thousand people. It usually happens in small ways and in one-on-one settings. First, I have to find someone—a mentor, a pastor, or a trusted and mature friend—who can maintain confidentiality and who understands the message of the Cross (i.e., that we are radically accepted even in the midst of our worst sinfulness). The next step is at once simple and excruciatingly difficult: I meet with that brother or sister, look him or her in the eye, and tell the story of my sin. Hopefully my brother or sister won't excuse me or shame me. He or she will just listen. And then my "confessor" can pronounce God's word of forgiveness (for example, by reading 1 John 1:6–2:2; Romans 5:6-11; or Hebrews 10:17). As my friend merely listens to my confession, God is already piercing my heart with sorrow and a holy desire, delivering me from the darkness of secrecy and shame.

This was one of my barriers to true penthos: I viewed it as a private, individualistic, spiritual transaction between me and God alone. But true repentance always takes place in community. It isn't just a solo act. That's why as a pastor I insist that we say our weekly prayers of confession together. We confess together and we repent together. Repentance shouldn't drive us to loneliness and isolation; it should drive us deeper into community.

Making Progress in the School of Repentance

More than forty years ago Mrs. Floaten wrote on my kindergarten report card, "Matt has been making good progress." When God sends me back to the school of repentance, I feel like I am moving backward; actually, I am making progress. I am starting to grasp the spring of joy that flowed in the heart of a holy fool like Francis of Assisi. After long days of weeping in his mountain hideout, Francis reappeared, "his face illumined by a smile that said it all: grace rediscovered, the heart surrendered to joy and love, especially love. The greatest sinner was becoming the greatest lover in the world."[13]

Six months into the initial shock of my journey into repentance, the gift of tears lessened, but as the holy fools had promised, the tears softened my heart. In a strange way, I felt exposed, broken, empty-handed, and poor—more so than I had ever felt in my life—but I also felt embraced, healed, and lavishly loved by God. The wild bull of God's grace had pierced and gripped my heart. But in that soul-shattering goring, God came crashing into my life like a "wild tormented lover," restoring my sight, healing my brokenness, and lavishing me with his grace.

QUESTIONS FOR REFLECTION

Have you ever entered into a season of deep repentance? What did that look like in your life? How did it start? What were the fruits of your season of repentance?

What did the old man in the desert mean when he said, "Truly, I am not sure whether I have even begun to repent"?

What did the holy fools mean by the phrase "the gift of tears"? Why are tears a gift? Do you think that tears are always necessary in our process of repentance?

"The opposite of repentance isn't plastic happiness or positive self-esteem; it's a hard heart." What does the Bible mean by having a hard heart? What makes your heart grow hard (or soft) toward God and other people?

Read Luke 15:7, 10, and 22-24. Notice the threefold declaration of joy in the midst of or because of repentance. How and why does repentance lead to joy? Does your repentance lead to joy? What is our repentance missing if joy is lacking?

CHAPTER 5

Engaging Our Brokenness

If we know how great is the love of Jesus for us, we will never be afraid to go to Him in all our poverty, all our weakness, all our spiritual wretchedness. . . . We will prefer to come to Him poor and helpless. We will never be ashamed of our distress.

THOMAS MERTON

ABOUT FIFTEEN YEARS AGO, a friend told me about a simple but beautifully written book called *The Power of the Powerless* by Christopher de Vinck. It's the true story of Christopher and his older brother Oliver. Oliver was born with birth defects so severe that many people called him a vegetable. According to Christopher, "I grew up in a house where my brother was on his back in his bed for thirty-two years, in the same corner of the room, under the same window, beside the same yellow walls. He was blind, mute. His legs were twisted. He didn't have strength to lift his head or the intelligence to learn anything. Oliver was born with severe brain damage that left him and his body in a permanent state of helplessness."[1]

But as Christopher tells the story of his brother's life, we realize that Oliver—weak, mute, helpless—possessed power to change the course of history. After Christopher's story was published in the *Wall Street Journal* and then republished in the *New York Post*, he started receiving letters from around the world. Even President Reagan sent a personal letter saying how much the story had changed him. Oliver's powerless life was influencing some of the most powerful people on the planet! Christopher concluded, "As a teacher, I spend many hours preparing lessons, hoping that I can influence my students. . . . Thousands of books are printed each year with the hope that the authors can move people to action. . . . Oliver could do absolutely nothing except breathe, sleep, eat, and yet he was responsible for action, love, courage, insight."[2]

I didn't read the book when my friend recommended it a long time ago, and I'm glad I waited fifteen years. I wouldn't have understood it then (although in my arrogance I would have thought I did). I needed to take a long, slow journey into the center of my own brokenness and powerlessness. But fifteen years later when I read De Vinck's story, I finally grasped a central principle of holy folly: strength in weakness. God's power flows into and then gushes out of human vulnerability. It's the principle of engaging our brokenness, running into it rather than fleeing it or denying it, but then finding true strength—God's strength—smack in the middle of our brokenness.

The Story of Brokenness

I'm not sure why God has organized the spiritual life around this principle of brokenness. I just know that it's woven into the larger story found in the Bible. It's an odd and foolish plotline: God possesses unlimited power, but for some reason he seems to enjoy working through weakness and brokenness. Out of the chaos of noncreation, God creates a world and it's "very good" (Genesis 1). Out of the mess of sin and rebellion, God promises to send a Redeemer (see Genesis 3:15). Out of the failed dreams of a childless couple (Abraham and Sarah), God initiates his surprising, world-saving plan (see Genesis 12–15). Out of the broken history of his flawed people, God makes a covenant of love (see Exodus 24). Out of a huge army, God whittles the troops down until a mere handful of soldiers trust him for victory (see Judges 6–9). Out of a dead stump, God promises a new branch, a Messiah (see Isaiah 11:1-9). Out of broken bread and spilled wine, Jesus feeds our famished souls (see Luke 22:14-22). Out of a barbaric cross, God the Father triumphs over the bondage of sin, death, and despair (see Colossians 2:13-15). And out of a preposterous band of freaks and fools and ragged sinners, the Holy Spirit builds the church (see 1 Corinthians 1:26-31).

As I started to notice God's quirky method of working through rather than around human brokenness, I was especially drawn to two biblical characters: King Jehoshaphat and the apostle Paul. Jehoshaphat's story is tucked in the Old Testament book of 2 Chronicles, chapter 20. As the king of Israel, Jehoshaphat faced a desperate situation: Three armies had combined to attack and decimate his people. It's a classic scene of brokenness and even desperation, but it also contains the possibility of God's power intervening. So as his heart melted with fear, Jehoshaphat prayed. "Look down here, God," he said (my paraphrase). "We're struggling and there's a horde of people trying to kill us and I don't know what you're up to, but could you just help us?"

I love this prayer because it's so utterly desperate. Some people have the assumption that as you grow in faith your prayers will become more calm, more respectable, and less desperate and urgent. That's not true. The best prayers are prayers from desperate and broken places. God would rather have a scorching-hot, angry, urgent groan from a holy fool than a smooth and respectable but ice-cold prayer from a super-Christian.

Then at the end of his prayer, Jehoshaphat confessed his utter human brokenness: "We are powerless against this mighty army that is about to attack us. We do not know what to do, but we are looking to you for help" (2 Chronicles 20:12). Kings and important people usually don't pray from broken places. Powerful, competent, intact (that is, nonbroken) people usually talk like this: "Well, folks, things are spiraling out of control and it looks bleak, but don't worry because we're analyzing the situation, our best people are now working on it, and very soon we'll reveal our brilliant five-year plan for success in these challenging circumstances." Instead, King Jehoshaphat stood up before his entire nation and admitted, in essence, "I'm the king, but I have no idea what to do. I'm totally lost and confused. Nothing is working right. We have no power to face this and we do not know what to do." But it's out of this confession of brokenness that God unleashed his power for good. As they turned to God in their desperation, Israel didn't even have to fight; the three armies turned inward and annihilated each other.

The apostle Paul serves as another prime example of the power of the powerless, the glory of finding strength in weakness. As he wrote to the new believers in the port city of Corinth, Paul knew that he was addressing an image-conscious, status-obsessed crowd that craved spiritual leaders who would dazzle them with religious slickness. Instead, they got Paul, a man littered with brokenness. Like the Grinch, he wouldn't be touched by most churches today with a thirty-nine-and-a-half-foot pole. By his own admission, Paul was at best a mediocre public speaker. On one occasion, as "Paul spoke on and on" (as Acts 20:9 delicately says of Paul's speaking ability), some kid from the youth group dozed off and plummeted out the window, falling three stories and cracking his head open. Nobody remembered Paul's slick sermon outline; all they could talk about was the dead kid who came back to life. Paul confessed that he came to the church in Corinth "in weakness—timid and trembling" (1 Corinthians 2:3). He may have had physical deformities, perhaps a constantly oozing eye. Rioting, turmoil, and jail sentences seemed to dog Paul's steps. He was the "worst of sinners"—not second place, but the gold-medal winner of broken, screwed-up people everywhere (see 1 Timothy 1:13-16).

But through a principle known as holy folly, God subverts and disrupts all our cherished assumptions of true power. It's precisely at the intersection of our weaknesses, the places where we feel much trembling, that the gospel blazes forth in the world. Paul would describe his own spiritual life in these unforgettable words: God's "power is made perfect in weakness" (see 2 Corinthians 12:9-10, NIV). Paul didn't mind being a holy fool. He even bragged about his weakness. As a result, Paul the broken man also became Paul the powerful man.

There are contemporary stories of the power of the powerless too. For instance, my friend Dave knows about weakness and brokenness. He lives in those things every day. About twenty years ago, by his own admission, Dave was breezing through life with brashness, competence, and "spiritual maturity." Weakness and brokenness were merely quaint, archaic concepts to Dave, until the doctors diagnosed him with an aggressive form of multiple sclerosis. Now confined to a wheel-chair, Dave shines with humility, gentleness, and peace. He's a broken man, a weak man in every sense of the word, but he also exudes a quiet strength and an absurd joy. God's power leaks through the cracks of his weakness and brokenness. David qualifies to join God's band of holy fools.

Power in Brokenness

Brokenness doesn't just imply that I'm "damaged" because life has victimized me. In the Christian story, my brokenness means that life has shattered me, but it also means that I have contributed to my own brokenness—and to the world's brokenness. In other words, I'm not just a victim of life's gusts; I'm also a rebel and fugitive. Every shattered piece of my life is still marked with the Master's beauty, but I'm not whole. Whatever I am, I'm not what I was made to be. I'm in pieces. Stated less delicately, I am, at least in part, a screwed-up human being.

And it gets even worse, because, according to the biblical story, I live in a broken world. One of the central themes of the Christian story found in the Bible is what theologians call "the fall of man" or "total depravity." Don't let the labels scare you. They just mean that although we're glorious creatures made in the image of God, every human being on this planet is also deeply flawed. Total depravity doesn't mean that every part of me is as bad as it could be. It just means that all my attitudes, actions, and even my deepest and most spiritual thoughts and aspirations are bent and flawed toward sin.

The Academy Award–winning move *Crash* contains a powerful scene about total depravity. Throughout the movie a white rookie cop consistently resists the blatant racism in his police department. He's young and idealistic and innocent, and he wants to conquer the evil of hatred and prejudice. He's utterly convinced that his innocent heart will prevail. But toward the end of the movie, while he's off duty, he picks up a young black hitchhiker. The black kid pulls out a small figurine designed to stick on a dashboard, but the white cop assumes it's a gun, so he shoots and kills his passenger. In utter horror and panic, the cop drives his car to an abandoned lot and sets it ablaze. As the flames ascend from the car (with the dead black youth inside), we watch the once-idealistic cop walking away, singed by his own dead dreams. His innocence is permanently stained by depravity.

This concept of depravity sounds depressing, but it actually flows into the other core element of brokenness: power. This power—God's power—has been released into our powerlessness. When we look at our brokenness, we don't just throw our hands in the air and say, "I'm a total loser; I quit." Not at all. Brokenness also means finding *strength* in our weakness. It isn't just being shattered; it's finding *wholeness* in Christ. It's interesting that the New Testament uses the Greek word *dunamis*, or power, forty-one times, but it's often combined with the word *asthenia*, or weakness. Power and weakness link together in an inseparable bond.[3] God wants to share his power with us. God longs to plant and cultivate real strength in us, but it often grows in the soil of our weakness.

The power of the powerless isn't a negative message. This God of power wants to pour his strength into broken human recipients, empowering us to live with love and courage, to enter into the mess of a frightening world, to forgive and be forgiven, to face our own sin and darkness, to live with joy and thanksgiving, to endure suffering. God is looking for a people who will receive and then display his power. And he *will* find them. But only the humble, the open, the empty-handed, and the broken will receive his power.

If he finds our hands full or our lives preoccupied with our own self-importance, he won't give us what we don't want.

One of my favorite holy fools, the English reformer John Wesley, experienced the power of the powerless. More than two hundred years ago, as a brash young man, he ventured from England to serve as a missionary in South Carolina. While he was in America he fell in love and proposed to a local woman. After Wesley panicked and broke off the engagement, the enraged father of the bride-to-be threatened to beat Wesley to a pulp, so John panicked again and bolted back to England. On the voyage home John froze in fear as the ship nearly sank. But a bunch of wildly happy Christ followers kept singing hymns as the ship threatened to plummet into the sea.

The ship eventually made it back to England, but this series of failures and weaknesses left John a deeply broken man. Shortly after these debacles, God spoke to John at a Bible study, and he "felt his heart strangely warmed." From that point on, John Wesley the broken man started to become John Wesley the holy fool. Over the years he challenged the religious establishment, preached to enraged mobs of people, helped thousands of people come to Christ, started a small-group movement, fed the hungry, healed the sick, and even encouraged a young politician named William Wilberforce to abolish the slave trade in England. But Wesley never forgot the principle of holy folly: the power of the powerless, the strength of God in our weakness, the wholeness in our brokenness.

I'll never forget nearly twenty years ago when an Anglican priest named William laid his hands on my forehead and prayed for the strength of the Holy Spirit to fill me and empower me. At that point in my life, I was so broken and weak. I felt inferior and inadequate. But through an unlikely source—William's touch and voice—the living God spoke truth into my heart. As William prayed for power to ignite my powerlessness, I had a clear image enter my mind: An oak tree had just been planted in my heart. It was strong and true; it even *felt* solid inside my chest. And I had the distinct impression that it would continue to grow tall and straight. For twenty years it has been growing inside my soul, slowly (painfully so for others around me) settling into the core of my identity. William's simple, daring prayer became my initiation into the power of the powerless.

Fleeing Our Brokenness

Most of us find the brokenness in our world and in our lives so unpleasant that we try to flee from it, opting for denial instead. The brilliant philosopher Blaise Pascal claimed that since we can't cure "death, wretchedness and ignorance," we've developed all kinds of slick diversions to avoid even thinking about our brokenness.[4] In more spiritual circles, denial takes a decidedly religious twist as we spout clichés or reduce the spiritual quest to a series of tidy steps. Before we know it, entire Christian communities are acting out an unwritten script pretending we've moved beyond our brokenness—or we just take a safer route and flee community altogether.

A few months ago a young man named Jim (a new Christian) sent me an e-mail recounting a sad tale of brokenness. After returning from a mission trip in which he served God by working with AIDS orphans, some of the most broken people on the planet, Jim's life quickly shattered. His girlfriend dumped him, his employer fired him, his mother booted him out of the house, and just for good measure, his church disowned him. With searing honesty, Jim concluded his story of brokenness by saying, "In short, life really stinks right now."

I couldn't respond to his e-mail for two weeks. So when I finally asked for an update on his life, Jim replied, "Well, nothing has changed, but after talking it over with a few more mature Christian friends, I just decided to turn everything over to God and accept everything in my life as God's perfect will." I didn't disagree with this theology, but it seemed too hollow and unreal. I wrote back and told Jim that I preferred his "life really stinks" e-mail. (There was more later, of course, but that was my initial reaction.)

I can't blame Jim; appearing weak is embarrassing and painful. If people really knew the depths of my brokenness, they might turn away in disgust. So early in our lives we develop sophisticated and largely undetected strategies for hiding our broken pieces. Psychologists call these defense mechanisms. Spiritual writers sometimes refer to them as false selves. For example, I don't want you to see parts of my real self—the incompetent, aching, angry, and lustful sinner—so I artfully present my false self—the super-nice, efficient, spiritually intact pastor. Like an open wound on the flesh, brokenness is just too messy and ugly. We'd rather numb it, blunt it, and escape it.

Facing Our Brokenness

In sharp contrast to our revulsion to weakness, the holy fools engaged brokenness with passionate intensity. They never tried to create more brokenness; they just refused to wallow in denial and unreality. "There is no greater disaster in the spiritual life," warned Thomas Merton, "than to be immersed in unreality. . . . When our life feeds on unreality, it must starve."[5] So the holy fools faced reality with all its beauty and cracks, wonder and flaws. Remember, this is not just the story of powerlessness but of *power in our weakness.* So as we face our weakness, God unleashes his power in our lives.

In the tradition of holy folly, we witness the courage to face our brokenness from an unlikely and marginal source—a blind beggar named Bartimaeus. This simple Gospel story, focusing on a minor hero of the spiritual journey, throbs with all the elements of holy folly—subversion, surprise, and even humor. The neat, clean, proper, and competent religious people just don't get it. But Bartimaeus—messy, poor, blind, and uncouth—attracts Jesus and finds healing.

According to Mark's account, Jesus, the disciples, and a "large crowd" encountered Bartimaeus as they were exiting Jericho (see Mark 10:46-52). Apparently no one had told Bartimaeus how to behave in church, so he shouted incessantly, "Jesus, Son of David, have mercy on me!" The spiritually competent members of Jesus' entourage offered "helpful" insights for Bartimaeus's request: "Would you just shut up and get lost?" they told him, in so many words. But as Bartimaeus pursued Jesus with reckless intensity, he shouted even louder, "Son of David, have mercy on me!" He knew he was a broken man, but he ached for wholeness.

Jesus stopped and noticed this broken, desperate man, because that's the way God works: His power surges into empty, weak places. "Cheer up," the crowd told Bartimaeus. "He's calling you." Bartimaeus flung aside his ragged cloak, jumped to his feet, and stumbled forward to meet Jesus (see verse 50). "What do you want me to do for you?" Jesus asked. "Rabbi," he exclaimed with holy boldness, "I want to see." Jesus responded with simplicity, "Go, for your faith has healed you." The entourage could only gape in wonder as the ragged, broken outcast danced and followed Jesus down the street.

Bartimaeus the holy fool faced and engaged his brokenness. With unflinching courage, he admitted the reality of his situation:

He was blind, poor, and uncouth. He didn't pretend to be in a better place. And he certainly didn't worry about impressing the crowd of "competent" and "whole" people who swarmed around Jesus. Instead, with audacious hope, he came to Jesus, the source of healing and power.

The Basis for Intimacy with God

Bartimaeus demonstrated one of the beautiful benefits of holy folly: Facing our brokenness draws us into intimacy with God the Father. Unfortunately, that's not the way we usually think about it. Brokenness usually causes a great deal of shame and fear. What if others find out? Will they reject me? Given the depths of our fear and shame, no wonder we run from God and others whenever we feel broken inside.

When I was about ten years old, my father, who worked as a medical doctor, received a beautiful musical globe from one of his patients. The base could be held in one hand while the globe was wound with the other to make the brilliant blue globe slowly spin and play music. I remember my dad proudly showing it to the rest of the family, gently cautioning us to use it only with extreme care. I loved my dad, but I knew more about musical globes than he did. So time and again I wound the ball farther and farther so the music would play longer and longer, until I wound the ball so far that it snapped and separated from the base. As I held a piece of his gift in each hand, a hot, terrifying shame washed over my soul. I had broken my dad's beautiful blue globe. So I hid the broken pieces under my shirt and slunk up to my room, hiding for hours behind my closet door.

We do the same thing in our relationship with God. According to the biblical story, human beings have a long history of hiding behind closet doors when they break God's stuff. When Adam and Eve broke the clear word of God and ate the forbidden fruit, they ran and hid. "Where are you?" God called out to them. Adam responded sheepishly, "I hid. I was afraid because I was naked" (Genesis 3:9-10). Adam's story is our story: The fear of our brokenness causes us to run and hide.

But the God of Genesis, who is the same God we see in the person of Jesus, pursues us with fierce mercy. God sought and found Adam and Eve in the Garden. God found Bartimaeus by the side of the road. We need the story of holy folly to remind us that God doesn't embrace us when we've finally put ourselves back together and shed every last trace of brokenness. No, he seeks us out and embraces us in the midst of our brokenness. Surprisingly, Jesus moved toward the messiness of Bartimaeus rather than toward the apparent spiritual intactness of the crowd around him.

No one demonstrated the intimacy of brokenness better than the apostle Paul. Paul seemed to face the depth of his brokenness on a daily basis. He called himself not just a sinner but the "the worst of sinners," the maestro, the big kahuna, the grand master of sinners (1 Timothy 1:16, NIV). Paul faced reality and declared the simple facts of his life: "I was once a blasphemer and a persecutor and a violent man" (1 Timothy 1:13, NIV). And yet, rather than run away from Christ, Paul headed straight into his arms of mercy: "The grace of our Lord was poured out on me abundantly, along with the faith and love that are in Christ Jesus. . . . Christ Jesus came into the world to save sinners" (1 Timothy 1:14-15, NIV). If that's why he came, then why would we run away from him? If he entered our broken world and at the cross absorbed into his body all the sharp, jagged pieces of our brokenness and even the "sins of all the world" (1 John 2:2), why would we want to hide? We call this concept "justification by faith."

It simply means that Jesus' life, death, and resurrection weave a story about a God who embraces us in the midst of our shattered pieces, not after we tidy up the mess.

No wonder Thomas Merton could write, "If we know how great is the love of Jesus for us, we will never be afraid to go to Him in all our poverty, all our weakness, all our spiritual wretchedness and infirmity. Indeed, when we understand the true nature of His love for us, we will prefer to come to Him poor and helpless. We will never be ashamed of our distress."[6] When we understand who Christ is and what he has done on our behalf, we will, like Bartimaeus, stand up rather than cower in fear, fling off our coat rather than cover our nakedness, and run to Jesus rather than slink away in shame.

The Basis for Community

God also uses the principle of strength in weakness to form the basis for the true community called the church. The French painter Georges Rouault beautifully conveys this biblical basis for community. Rouault (1871–1958) spent most of his life in the impoverished outskirts of Paris, where circuses often breezed into town. Taking childlike delight in the clowns, Rouault devoted more than sixty of his nearly five hundred paintings to clowns. His painting entitled *The Injured Clown* captures a scene with a small community of clowns who are helping an injured clown. The clown, whose costume and makeup represent intactness and invulnerability, has fallen. Like Christians, clowns presumably aren't supposed to fall. But this one has fallen hard, and he's wounded. In his brokenness and neediness, the injured clown leans on his friends who shelter him as they walk his wounded body to safety.[7]

With one picture, Rouault the master artist captured the basis for Christian community: Our friends transmit God's strength in our weakness. My holy fool friend Dave loves telling the story of a famous Scottish preacher who was paralyzed by his fear of heights. As life (or God) would have it, this broken man had to climb into the pulpit by ascending a huge, winding staircase. His fear was so overwhelming that the elders of the church had to grab him under the arms Sunday after Sunday and drag him to the top of the staircase so he could preach from the pulpit. After they carried him up the stairs, he preached with power and conviction. Because we are broken and wounded, we really do need each other. We are the injured clown, the terrified preacher who needs to be carried. And we are the healthy clowns and elders who need to carry our brothers and sisters.

Christian communities that engage brokenness pour forth mercy, especially to the weak and vulnerable members of our human family. Brokenness softens hearts and causes justice and mercy to flow like a fountain. Jean Vanier, the founder of the L'Arche communities for the severely mentally handicapped, shares his story of allowing Christ's mercy to flow through his brokenness. When he started living with two handicapped young men, he discovered the hardness in his heart: "I saw forces of hate rising up inside of me, and the capacity to hurt someone who was weak and was provoking me. . . . I did not want to admit all the garbage inside me." After struggling with his own brokenness, Vanier made a startling discovery: "Jesus came to bring good news to the poor, not those who serve the poor! . . . The healing power in us will not come from our capacities and our riches, but in and through our poverty. We are called to discover that God can bring peace, compassion and love through *our* wounds."[8]

Part of a Grand Story

If you're anything like me, you resist this principle of holy folly. Most of us would rather keep running away from our weakness and spiritual poverty. But then we hit a wall (and we always will eventually), and we say, "I can't get over it; I can't get around it. I can't shake this addiction. I can't fix my marriage. I can't defeat death. I can't find love. I can't heal the sadness and loneliness in my heart. I can't right the world's wrongs by fighting injustice and racism and poverty, because there's selfishness in my heart. I can't get over my anger or my fear." And like Jehoshaphat we're forced to cry out to God, "We are powerless against this. . . . We do not know what to do."

Once again, God intends to lead us into something good and noble through our encounters with brokenness. The power of the powerless is woven into the grand story that God is writing for the entire cosmos. The apostle Paul peeled back the curtain of eternity and basically said, "This isn't just God's plan for my life and your life; it's God's plan for the entire universe. Through Christ, God will reconcile all things to himself" (see Colossians 1:20). It incorporates the story of my healing as a subplot, but the grand narrative swells with breathtaking majesty. God will take all the broken pieces of the universe and restore them.

It's a strange story, but as evidence of God's cosmic restoration process, the early followers of Jesus always pointed to the cross. At the cross, Jesus absorbed in his body all the broken shards of our wounded planet. "He made Him who knew no sin to be sin on our behalf," wrote the apostle Paul (2 Corinthians 5:21, NASB). Through Jesus, God will "reconcile to himself all things . . . by making peace through his blood, shed on the cross" (Colossians 1:20, NIV). Again, it appears so strange—such weakness, such folly! And yet, the New Testament argues, at the cross

God's weakness is "stronger than the greatest of human strength," and his foolishness is "wiser than the wisest of human plans" (1 Corinthians 1:25). Even God operates by the principle of strength through brokenness.

And flowing from his great work on the cross, God is now choosing broken people to participate in this cosmic renovation operation. In C. S. Lewis's startling image, we are treading Adam's dance backwards.[9] We're not finished yet. We're still broken, but Christ has flung open a door. Those who are in Christ, those who dare to walk through the door, have been ushered into a new creation (see 2 Corinthians 5:17). Through him we are on the way back to wholeness and intactness. Broken people find something good and pure and strong growing deep inside: the healing power of Jesus.

One of the most important mentors in my life, a man named C. Philip Hinerman, or just "Doc" for short, taught me some profound lessons about the power of the powerless. For nearly thirty years Doc had a successful ministry at a large multiethnic church in south Minneapolis. A brilliant speaker, Doc was nationally known for his creative outreach to the community and for his commitment to bring blacks and whites together during tense times. Doc achieved success and influence and even fame. For five years during my days at seminary, I sat under Doc's leadership and teaching. And then for another twelve years Doc served as a pastoral mentor and spiritual father in my life. During those years I noted and admired Doc's ascent and his success.

But then on his seventieth birthday, Doc was forced to retire from his church in Minnesota, so he moved to North Carolina and became the senior pastor of a large church there. He continued with his bold preaching, his commitment to racial unity, and his outreach to the neighborhood of the local church. But this time Doc encountered a powerful group of church folks who didn't appreciate his approach to church life. They accused him of dangerous ministry techniques. They attacked his character, accusing him of laziness because he took a nap every afternoon. (They didn't know—and Doc never told them—that he needed a nap because he arose between 4:00 and 5:00 a.m. so he could pray for two hours.) After a two-year battle, they got Doc fired.

At age seventy-two, Doc was no longer the successful, popular, famous pastor. His wife, Adora, was bedridden with rheumatoid arthritis. I didn't know it at the time, but Doc was preparing for the greatest battles of his life. In one season he would deal with his wife's frailty and illness, his own sense of failure (he had never failed at a church before), his isolation from his loved ones in Minneapolis, and his own age and physical weakness—and of course the accompanying discouragement and doubt as well. And at the same time he was laying the foundation for his greatest legacy. Looking back on it now, in his early days in Minneapolis, Doc taught me some profound lessons about the ascent into power. But in these later days, Doc taught me even more profound lessons about the power of the powerless.

In the midst of his weakness, God's power sustained Doc. He continued loving his wife, forgiving his enemies, and pouring out his life for the hundreds of young men and women who called Doc their spiritual mentor or father. On Saturday mornings Doc would meet these young people for breakfast. Everyone knew Doc's standard breakfast for these meetings: a cup of coffee and a caramel roll with pecans. Over his cup of coffee, Doc would ask questions and listen and encourage and challenge us. Over his nearly thirty years as a pastor, he mentored dozens if not hundreds of young men to enter the pastorate or other professions where they could make an impact in business, missions, medicine, the arts, and music. Doc's wife died a few years after their move to North Carolina, and then Doc died at the age of seventy-five.

Doc, the broken man, never gave up. But it wasn't just Doc or Doc's strength that sustained him. In his last days he lived the secret of the holy fools: the power of the powerless. "We ourselves are like fragile clay jars containing this great treasure," the apostle Paul wrote. "This makes it clear that our great power is from God, not from ourselves" (2 Corinthians 4:7).

QUESTIONS FOR REFLECTION

In the context of the biblical story as a whole, what do you think it means to be truly broken? Can you think of people in the Bible or in your own life who are examples of brokenness or strength out of weakness?

Read the story of Bartimaeus in Mark 10:46-52. How does his encounter with Jesus demonstrate the reality of God's power in our weakness?

Have you ever had a distinct moment of finding God's strength in your weakness? What happened, and what was the fruit of that moment?

"Christian communities that engage brokenness pour forth mercy, especially to the weak and vulnerable members of our human family. Brokenness softens hearts and causes justice and mercy to flow like a fountain." Based on this description, how well are you—or your church, your small group, or your family—caring for the weak and vulnerable?

Read 1 Corinthians 2:1-5. In what areas of your life do you, like the apostle Paul, feel "timid and trembling"? Spend some time asking God to turn your weakness into an opportunity to encounter his strength.

AWAKENING TO A LIFE
OF DISCIPLINE

CHAPTER 6

Training as an Athlete of God

To be at home with God, so that one associates with Him gladly and feels the joy of His presence . . . like every other serious matter, requires practice. It must be willed and carried out with much self-conquest, again and again.

ROMANO GUARDINI

TWENTY-FIVE YEARS AGO I was a finely tuned athletic machine. At the age of nineteen, I could run a five-minute mile, slam-dunk a basketball, sprint around a baseball diamond, and pummel the opposition in a violent game of tackle football. The next morning I'd wake up fully prepared to give and receive more athletic abuse. Last month I played a game of half-court basketball and found myself sucking wind within five minutes. I couldn't dunk a Nerf ball on the kiddie hoop. I had a similar experience on our church's softball team: While trying to stretch a single into a double, my left hamstring exploded like a small land mine. Now it pops and rips at least once a year.

I can chock up some of this to age. I'm just getting older, and in the words of the great African novelist Chinua Achebe, "Things fall apart." So I'm falling apart—I can't control that. But I'm convinced that age is only 20 percent of the problem; the other 80 percent is definitely within my control. I don't train anymore. I don't go to the gym. I don't work out. I don't practice my jumps or dives or shots or throws. My "training regimen" consists of walking our beagle in the backyard until he pees.

With profound humility, I realize that I am no longer an athlete. Real athletes may miss shots and pull hamstrings and even deteriorate with age, but there is one nonnegotiable requirement for real athletes: They actually train. A real athlete develops a regimen of exercises, crunches, stretches, shots, and kicks, and he sticks with it until his body obeys his mind. The key is the practice, a routine of practice that is challenging, consistent, persistent, and focused on a long-range goal.

The Holy Fools: Athletes for God

Based on my falling-apart, training-free role as an ex-athlete, it didn't surprise me that many of the holy fools were called "athletes of God." I quickly discovered that they actually practiced a rigorous spiritual routine—and stuck with it. They believed that the spiritual life, just like the physical life, requires the commitment of an athlete. Their disciplined routine focused on a long-range goal: Christlike freedom and holiness. The technical name for their spiritual practice is *asceticism*, and their commitment to an ascetic lifestyle was embedded in the core of their life in Christ.

In the early fourth century, for instance, just as the Christian faith had gained social and political acceptance, a new movement emerged in the early church. Men and women turned their backs on the cozy, diluted Christianity of their day, trekking into the harsh, lonely deserts of Egypt and Palestine. Some lived alone. Others banded together into small communities of fellow pilgrims. All of them developed a routine of spiritual practices that consisted of silence, solitude, fasting, simple labor, Scripture meditation, radical hospitality, and compassion.

Most historians point to a man named Antony as the pivotal leader in this desert movement. According to a biography written in the fourth century by a contemporary of Antony's named Athanasius, he was born into a wealthy Christian family and started his journey with Christ sitting in church and listening to the Gospel reading. When he heard the story of the rich young leader (see Luke 18:18-30), Antony took the message to heart, selling everything and settling in an abandoned fort in the desert. For twenty years he battled demons through the night, denied himself food, pummeled his body, memorized the Bible, prayed in his cell, and tended his small garden.

Basket-Weaving Wild Men

I must confess that the ascetic aspect of the holy fools didn't exactly rouse my heart. Initially I found it utterly foreign and even repugnant. So a bunch of emaciated wild men trekked into the desert, wove their baskets (which they sold to benefit the poor), constantly fasted or at best subsisted on bread and oil and water, and then engaged demonic spirits in rounds of intense spiritual warfare. And just what was the point of that? So although my spiritual life—marked by a pampered, comfortable, nonascetic lifestyle—was disintegrating, I could still judge the early holy fools and conclude that their asceticism was utterly irrelevant and repulsive.

Why did I react so strongly? First of all, as I investigated the holy fools, I noticed that in their athleticism for God they sometimes missed a fundamental truth of Christian theology: the goodness of creation. Some holy fools, including Antony, acted like they hated their bodies. For some reason I couldn't picture Antony enjoying a juicy steak with mashed potatoes, chocolate mousse, and a robust glass of sauvignon. Nor could I see him sitting beside his wife in a movie theater chomping on buttered popcorn. I happen to like juicy steaks, mashed potatoes, movies, buttered popcorn—and my wife, of course—and I have a hunch that God enjoys my enjoyment.

But my second objection was more personal and less noble: I've always resented the self-denial and discipline involved in asceticism. By the time my occasional twenty-four-hour fasts were over, I wanted to bolt home and stuff my face with food until I'd consumed twice the calories I'd just denied myself. In an affluent and permissive age, it's tough to view myself as a spiritual athlete—and I don't know many followers of Christ who do.

I noticed with smug satisfaction that Thomas Merton had the same response. "Asceticism!" he wrote with derision. "The word had so far stood for a kind of weird and ugly perversion of nature, the masochism of men who had gone crazy in a warped and unjust society. . . . Those things had never succeeded in giving me anything but gooseflesh."[1]

In spite of their extreme approach, I realized that these ascetic holy fools had a perspective I needed to hear. As is often the case with the desert fathers, this perspective came crashing into my life through a simple story. A fourth-century desert father named Abba Sisoes once begged his protégé, "Tell me what you see in me and in turn I will tell you what I see in you." (I just love their simple honesty.) The young man said, "You are good in soul, but a little harsh." Abba Sisoes replied to the younger man, "And you are good but your soul is not tough."[2] I can see myself—and in one sense, my entire generation—in the young man. In my approach to the spiritual disciplines I may be "good" (I do practice some of them some of the time), but I am not "tough" (I am inconsistent, undisciplined, and just plain "out of shape"). I need some of their ancient spiritual toughness and rigor.

Not So Weird, After All

In order to develop a twenty-first-century, creation-affirming, evangelical asceticism, I had to deconstruct my intellectual misconceptions and emotional revulsion. Certainly, bizarre forms of self-denial appeared early in the church's life. The apostle Paul wasn't impressed. Not one to mince words, Paul called these extremists "hypocrites and liars" and claimed that their creation-denying practices actually came from deceptive spirits and demons (see 1 Timothy 4:1-2). Such people are not only misguided, they have severed their lives from the head, Jesus (see Colossians 2:16-19).

Paul's main argument, which has been the guiding principle for two thousand years of Christian spirituality, was a foundational Jewish viewpoint: Creation is good. In other words, God created things—bagels with cream cheese, barbecued chicken wings, fresh-brewed Kona coffee, marriage, friendship, music, dance, and art—to be received with thanksgiving. Why? "Since *everything*

God created is good, we should not reject *any* of it but receive it with thanks" (1 Timothy 4:4, emphasis mine). Or as C. S. Lewis once said, "[God] likes matter. He invented it."[3] I would also add that Jesus likes bodies; he became a body. And Jesus likes food; he ate it often enough. In order to embrace a balanced asceticism, we must affirm and even delight in God's good creation.

I noticed that some of the holy fools severed their good Jewish roots. But others managed to avoid an unbiblical distortion of asceticism, remaining attached to Jesus and the good creation. I learned that the Greek root for asceticism, *askesis*, never carried the baggage of extremism; it simply referred to the training, discipline, and exercise required for athletic competition. Paul applied the word to his spiritual journey in Christ: "I always try [or exercise—the Greek word comes from *askesis*] to maintain a clear conscience before God and all people" (Acts 24:16). When Paul wrote to a young pastor named Timothy, he urged him to "train yourself to be godly" (1 Timothy 4:7). Basically this translates to "hit the gym of godliness and work out." The Bible seems to delight in athletic images: running a race (see Philippians 3:12-14 and Hebrews 12:1-2), boxing (see 1 Corinthians 9:26), wrestling (see Ephesians 6:12, KJV).

The asceticism required for the spiritual journey is a normal part of life. In this sense, there is nothing strange or repulsive about asceticism. A few weeks ago at my thirteen-year-old son's soccer meeting, Coach Mark lectured the parents about the athletes' need for an ascetic lifestyle. "This team will not tolerate drinking, smoking, and sex. If your sons want to train as athletes, they have to learn to control their bodies." I kept waiting for the praise team to start singing and the ushers to come forward for the offering, but I wasn't in church. I was still at the Stony Brook Cyclones parent-coach meeting. *Wow,* I thought, *is this the only place to preach about and expect a high level of asceticism?*

Actually, we practice askesis all the time. Flossing my teeth, dribbling a basketball, eating Grape-Nuts instead of sausage, cramming for a final exam, meditating on Scripture, withdrawing into silence and solitude, and fasting for a day—all of these things require askesis, a routine of behavior that is challenging, consistent, persistent, and focused on a long-range goal.

Viewed from this angle, there was nothing dreary, unnatural, or repulsive about asceticism. I started to see that askesis is part of normal Christianity. And once again, the holy fools had an important lesson for me. Granted, at times they pushed their askesis too far; we (or at least I), on the other hand, had slacked off on the notion of positive askesis that leads to growth. As a result, spiritually speaking (and please keep in mind, I am *only* speaking metaphorically here), I had become a fat, lazy, bald, middle-aged guy who perpetually sucked air, couldn't jump more than nine inches, and blew out my hamstring because I refused to train myself for godliness. (Once again, this statement has no bearing on my current physical condition.)

In a holy fools–inspired lifestyle, I found a model of askesis that could reverse this trend, training me for the spiritual journey in Christ. However, over the years I've also discovered two warnings inherent in ascetic practice. First, discipline by itself doesn't change us; only the power of the Holy Spirit can change a heart. Specific exercises merely open our lives to the ongoing work of the Holy Spirit. Love, joy, peace, goodness, etc.—these are fruit of the Holy Spirit, not fruit of my spiritual discipline (see Galatians 5:22-23). Second, askesis wasn't an end in itself for the holy fools, just as the end of lifting weights isn't looking in the mirror and admiring yourself. The holy fools' regimen of workouts prepared them to love well. Love God with all your heart and love your neighbor as yourself—according to Jesus that's the essence of the spiritual quest (see Matthew 22:37-39). Askesis will help you get there.

Abba Poemen, one of the masters of desert asceticism, always kept love—not competition or performance or severe discipline— at the forefront of the spiritual life. On one occasion a group of spiritual leaders approached Poemen and asked him, "When we see someone falling asleep during the services, should we rouse him so he will be watchful?" Poemen, who had devoted his life to practicing and training for Christlikeness, responded, "For my part, when I see someone falling asleep, I place his head on my knees and let him rest."[4] Asceticism doesn't make us harsh and rigid; instead, in the power of the Holy Spirit, it hones our bodies and minds so we can quickly and fluidly respond to the call of love.

Beginning Steps in the Ascetic Life

(Or how to live as a middle-class American ascetic who may never see a real desert)

Unfortunately, learning to love like Christ, just like getting in shape for a basketball team, doesn't just happen. From the holy fools I am slowly learning that loving well requires a life-long regimen of training. After years of pampering, my flabby self-will doesn't always respond. As a result, soul-deadening desires—greed, lust, anger, impatience, fear, arrogance—still enslave my heart. When left unchecked, these desires became like spoiled little brats, clamoring for attention and eventually taking over the household. American Christianity at large has many spoiled, untrained children (like me) wreaking havoc in churches throughout the land.

The solution for Antony and other holy fools was to embark on a journey to the desert. The holy fools found the desert to be a place of harsh terrain and severe limitation. But in the biblically inspired imagination, the desert—dry, brown, and hard—became their gym. The desert doesn't care about soothing egos or pampering the flesh's lust, greed, arrogance, and comfort. Instead, by stripping off unnecessary baggage and training us to run the race, the desert becomes the harsh but effective personal trainer of the spiritual life.

From the holy fools I am learning that the ascetic life often begins where I least expect it—right in the midst of my daily, ordinary routine. Unlike Antony, I can't pack up and hike into the desert for twenty years. I can't even go for a month. But even as a middle-class American ascetic wannabe, I don't need to go to the desert, because the desert will come to me. I am learning that by paying attention to my daily life, I find ample challenges to train me in spiritual maturity and askesis. These small deserts cross my path every time my needs are denied and my will is challenged.

Consider the simple inconvenience of waiting in line at a fast-food restaurant. Last summer a Spanish-speaking adolescent boy confused the orders at our local fast-food restaurant. Everyone had to wait at least four minutes instead of two minutes for their soft tacos and slimy fake-cheese nachos. Talk about murmuring in the wilderness! We were thoroughly miserable—but, hey, at least our outrage led to instant community. The guy in front of me, a six-foot-five beer-bellied hulk with a Stone Cold Steve Austin wrestling T-shirt, desperately wanted to get home and watch the latest cage match on pay-per-view. The sharply dressed woman at the head of the line needed to get back to the office. I was late for my son's soccer game. So in one accord we grumbled and threatened to boycott this particular restaurant chain. The guy with the wrestling T-shirt offered to pile-drive the poor kid into the counter.

Reflecting on this mini-desert in daily life from the perspective of the holy fools, this could have been an opportunity for askesis, for training and curbing the desires of anger and gluttony and selfishness (not to mention racist attitudes). I didn't get my way; I didn't get my tacos on my timetable. So what? I imagined Antony sitting on the dirty restaurant floor, weaving a basket and telling me, "Welcome to the desert, my friend. This trip may last only five minutes, but don't waste it. You have to wait. Waiting is a good thing. It challenges your nasty self-will, as displayed in your pushy, arrogant, impatient attitude. This taco-imposed desert—just like hundreds of other mini-deserts—could be God's invitation for you to grow in Christlike character. God is training you, little brother. So pull up a straw mat and enjoy your stop in the desert."

I realize this example may sound trite, but life is filled with similar examples of short trips to the desert. For instance, I started to see my marital situation as a desert experience. In some form or another, all marriages provide opportunities for askesis. Every time I don't get my way, every time my wife doesn't meet my needs the way I'd like her to, every time she confronts me with my sin, I get a taste of the desert.

Christian community can do the same thing. Every time we have to deal with people we find irritating, annoying, dull, slow, difficult, unreasonable, or downright sinful, God may be wooing us into the desert. Every time I have to submit to a decision that rubs me the wrong way or work through a conflict or listen to how I have wounded someone else, God may be training me in the spiritual life, denying my desires and building my muscles of patience, humility, and kindness.

Worship services themselves provide another opportunity for askesis. As a pastor, I know that slight alterations in worship styles often produce howls of protest. I also know that I can become a local folk hero and front-running candidate for president if I merely give people the "worship experience" they prefer. "Nice job with the worship, Pastor," usually means, "Thanks for doing it my way this time." But what if the worship service isn't a way to pander to my flesh? What if the worship service is a place of askesis? Perhaps the choruses, hymns, and prayers that I don't like are merely God-given tools to train me, trim my deep arrogance, and open me to love and life.

Again, these examples merely offer short treks into the desert, but my mentors, the holy fools, show me my need to hit the desert gym and grow strong and deep in Christ. The key is to pay attention to the small, "accidental" treks into the desert. We don't have to seek these out; they will come to us. But if I maintain the mind-set of an athlete-in-training, I will welcome these opportunities as additional chances to grow. God will use them to strip off excess baggage, training me to run the race and making me alive in Christ. Without these small treks into the desert—or making these treks without the attentiveness of an athlete—my spiritual life remains fat, lazy, and self-centered.

Intentional Athletic Practice

The holy fools had more to teach me about askesis than just how to respond to unintentional discipline. All real athletes know they must also develop an intentional regimen of training. Or in terms of desert spirituality, we must make some desert in our lives.

Sometimes the holy fools called this intentional regimen a "rule of life." A spiritual rule of life is simply a set of thoughtful, balanced spiritual disciplines that train us in godly character and spiritual awareness. It is a program for healthy spiritual living. That's why Simon Chan argues:

> Rule enables such people to plod along at the "slow and steady" pace to accomplish far more spiritually than those who rely on

unpredictable, sudden spurts of inspiration. To embrace a rule is to make a commitment to a certain pattern of living that helps reinforce desirable habits in the long term.[5]

The holy fools started developing a rule for the spiritual life that dates back to the fourth century. Some of the earliest Christian communities wrote their rules on the walls. The best-known rule for an entire community appeared nearly three hundred years later, when Saint Benedict planted his community in the midst of the social chaos swirling around him.[6] Benedict's rule revolved around a rhythm of prayer, work, and study. Benedict warned his spiritual athletes that his rule might produce an initial shock to the system ("it is bound to be narrow at the outset"), but this "little strictness" is only "in order to amend faults and safeguard love." The end result is not soul-deadening legalism but life and joy. "As we progress in the way of life and faith," promised Benedict, "we shall run on the path of God's commandments, our hearts overflowing with the inexpressible delight of love."[7]

As I listened to the holy fools, I realized that I had a rule—sort of. I often woke up, read some Bible verses, dragged myself to a weekly worship service, said grace before meals, and attended a small group. My rule was just inconsistent, haphazard, and individualistic.

How do we develop our own life-infusing rule of life for the spiritual journey? The holy fools seemed to reach across the generations, slap me gently but firmly across the face, and say, "Just start somewhere." I possess more "book knowledge" about spiritual disciplines than they did, but they were far more advanced in actually acting on their knowledge leading to joyful obedience.

Spiritual disciplines are the practices or habits that help us grow in our faith. The classic spiritual disciplines as outlined over twenty years ago in Richard Foster's book *Celebration of Discipline* include:

The inward disciplines: meditation, prayer, fasting, and study

The outward disciplines: simplicity, solitude, submission, and service

The corporate disciplines: confession, worship, guidance, and celebration[8]

I've known for years that Jesus, the ultimate holy fool, followed a simple pattern of engagement-ministry-solitude. Recently, my friend Steve Smith showed me every reference in the Gospels to Jesus' practice of withdrawing to find solitude and silence. Although the evidence was clear that Jesus withdrew on a regular basis, for some reason I still have a tough time with that solitude part. I think the holy fools might say, "Just do it. Don't think about it or whine about it or give me your excuses and rationalizations. Pull out your calendar and block out some dates right now."

I've suspected for years that there's something to this fasting thing. The whole point of asceticism is that there is a body-soul-spirit-mind connection. I can't continually pamper and gorge my body without a negative effect on my spiritual life. In contrast, occasionally denying myself practical necessities like food, disciplining my body, as Paul said (see 1 Corinthians 9:24-27), will help align my spiritual life more to God's perspective.

But the key is to start. Where or how? These are some ascetic possibilities I've tried over the years:

- Spend a day in silent prayer. There are hundreds of Christian retreat centers scattered throughout the United States and the world.[9] Most retreat centers provide a quiet room and quiet grounds to reflect and pray. For a modest donation or fee you can reserve a room for a day or two. (You could also borrow a cabin or, if you're more adventurous, a campsite.) Bring your Bible and a prayer journal and maybe one book to help you in your reflection and prayer. Don't try to accomplish too much on this prayer day. Just linger with God or "waste time" with Jesus. Read some Scripture, walk, listen, and take a nap if you get tired. Eat your meals in silence and without hurry. Actually taste every bite. If the community has set prayer times, join them. If the center offers spiritual direction, you might want to try at least one appointment with a trained spiritual director.

- Skip lunch once a week, giving the money to the poor and spending the time in prayer instead.

- Forgo food for a whole day once a month. Make the whole day a time of prayer—allow your hungry stomach to gurgle and pray to God all day long.

- Give up Starbucks coffee (or whatever brand that costs you way too much money) for Lent.

- Disconnect your extra cable channels for a season (not during March Madness, of course—the desert fathers also warned against *excessive* and *unreasonable* self-denial).

- Give up all forms of media (television, computers, radio, movies, newspapers) after 10:00 p.m. Spend the time in silence, listening for God's still, small voice.

- Memorize a psalm.

- Join a church or small group and actually submit to the spiritual leaders.

- Make the Sabbath a day of real rest. Change the rhythm of your Sabbaths.[10]

Certainly, none of these disciplines earn more favor with a God who operates by grace, but they do prepare my body and soul to respond to the call of love.

The question to ask is this: What are the disciplines that are helping to train me in Christlike living? Not just the ones I want to do someday or the ones I've read about. What are the actual, concrete, flesh-and-blood, body impacting habits and exercises that I practice on a regular and routine basis because I love God and I want to train myself to love others? What are they? Write them down. Next write down the exercises you'd like to start. And then do them.

The holy fools seemed to say not only, "Do it" but also, "Keep doing it"—for the next year and for the next ten years and, if it's a valuable discipline, for the next 1,400 years. My spirituality often tends toward the quick fix. I want shortcuts and gimmicks and instant results. But the holy fools remind me that I won't get in my top shape overnight. Sometimes it takes years. For instance, as our church prepared to plunge into our "40 Days of Purpose" campaign, I spent a night at the Saint Procopius Abbey near Chicago. When I joined the monks for morning and evening prayers as they chanted their way straight through the Psalter, it hit me that they've been doing this since Benedict's era. So much for forty days to spiritual maturity; these guys were on the 1,400 years of purpose track.

About fifteen years ago I started praying through the Psalms out loud, every verse, line by line, from Psalm 1 through Psalm 150 without skipping anything.[11] I've probably prayed through every psalm almost thirty times now. They're starting to grow on me, and they're starting to grow into me. They come to me in the middle of my "non-praying" times. They seep into my speech and my memory. On some days (it's rare but it happens) the Psalms seem to pray me more than I pray them. Again, this doesn't happen in forty days. So be patient, the holy fools would tell us. Keep practicing your spiritual disciplines. In regard to spiritual practices, keep at them for years—and that applies to worship and Sabbath keeping and fasting and any other spiritual discipline.

Finally, the holy fools would warn against a largely individualistic approach to askesis. On the one hand, the desert fathers seemed to emphasize their precious solitude and silence. One of the most famous lines from desert spirituality comes from the lips of Abba Moses, who said, "Go, sit in your cell and your cell will teach you everything." In other words, be alone with God. They practiced solitude.

But on the other hand, most of the stories about the holy fools deal with them in the context of community. For guys who were supposed to sit in their cells all day, they sure spent a lot of time yakking and telling stories with their buddies and total strangers. "Our life and death is with our neighbor" became the other most famous line in desert spirituality. So they practiced spiritual disciplines together—praying, fasting, weeping, fighting demons, providing meals, giving to the poor, memorizing Scripture together.[12]

The Results of Asceticism

When I first started playing basketball, I had to master a basic but difficult shot: the left-handed layup. On my first try I felt like a total klutz. Lining up my feet, jumping off my right foot, utilizing my opposite hand as I twisted in the air and tried to finesse a delicate touch—all these elements made it a tough maneuver. For the first few weeks, I had to work and grunt and sweat and concentrate. But after a while, I began to think less about getting it right and more about the joy of banking in a shot. I felt less like a klutz. Eventually I even felt like I was soaring (at least a tiny bit, anyway). Making a left-handed layup still required sweat and discipline and effort, but it also became enjoyable.

The spiritual disciplines work in much the same way. They may feel awkward at first and they may remain awkward for some time, but after a while you think less about the grunting and sweating and more about the joy of being with God. At first an hour of silence and solitude may seem painful, but then the hour starts to expand to a few hours and even half a day. Celebrating the Sabbath may feel inconvenient and clumsy, but as we keep practicing this simple discipline, it becomes delightful. As we learn the disciplines, as we sweat and practice, we may even feel like we're soaring with Jesus (well, a little bit, anyway).

That's what happened in the life of that early athlete for God named Antony. When he finally emerged after twenty years from his desert hideout, everyone commented on the effects of his spiritual regimen. "They were amazed to see that his body had maintained its former condition, neither fat . . . nor emaciated." At the age of 105, even his teeth were intact. His spiritual and emotional poise were even more impressive. After demons tortured his body and soul, Antony, the mighty warrior-athlete for God, triumphantly cried out to all the forces of hell and darkness, "Here I am—Antony! I do not run from your blows, for even if you give me more, nothing shall separate me from the love of Christ."

"The state of his soul was one of purity," Athanasius commented, "for it was neither restricted by grief, nor relaxed by pleasure. . . . He maintained utter equilibrium, like one guided by reason and steadfast in that which accords with nature."[13] Years of asceticism had trained Antony's heart and mind until he was truly centered in Christ. In Antony's life, God had answered the ascetic's prayer: *"We beg you, make us truly alive."*[14]

I'm discovering that my initial (and sometimes lingering) revulsion to asceticism was completely unfounded. I need askesis; I can't grow without it. Ultimately, genuine, God-centered, Spirit-guided, balanced askesis leads not to neurotic extremism but to freedom and security. Author and poet Kathleen Norris calls this the basic truth of asceticism: "It is a radical way of knowing who, what, and where you are in defiance of those powerful forces in society . . . that aim to make us forget. . . . Desert wisdom allows you to be at home wherever you are."[15] Or in Benedict's words from more than 1,400 years ago, asceticism helps us run in the way of God's commandments—something that requires practice, discipline, and training. But the end result is a heart "overflowing with the inexpressible delight of love."

QUESTIONS FOR REFLECTION

What is one part of your life that requires *askesis*? (This could be athletics, music, academics, or work.)

In your approach to spiritual disciplines, do you tend to be "a little harsh" or are you "not tough" enough?

"American Christianity at large has many spoiled, untrained children (like me) wreaking havoc in churches throughout the land." Where do you see our culture in this quote? Where do you see yourself?

What are your current desert opportunities—i.e., those places where you must say no to yourself or wait on God or others? How are you handling those desert experiences?

Look over the list of "ascetic possibilities" on pages 113–114. What is one possibility you would like to start or one you've already started but would like to keep developing?

CHAPTER 7

Praying like a Hermit

Most of us have an atrophied contemplative faculty. . . .
God is present to us, but we are not present to God. We
lack contemplativeness and because of this we lack a vital
experience of God.

RONALD ROLHEISER

Without true, deep contemplative aspirations, without a total
love for God and an uncompromising thirst for his truth,
religion tends in the end to become an opiate.

THOMAS MERTON

DEEP IN THE RUSSIAN FOREST, a tall, slender man with brilliant white hair stands on a rock, lifting his arms toward heaven and praying. Over and over again he utters the name of Jesus, imploring Christ's mercy for his own soul and all humankind. After praying for hours, he retreats to his simple hermitage for the night. During the long, silent evening, animals lovingly flock around his cabin, but otherwise he is alone in the darkness of the forest. Of his seventy-one years on this earth, nearly thirty of them will be spent in a hermit's hut. The Russian church reverently calls him Saint Seraphim of Sarov. He was a holy fool for Christ.

His birth name was Prokhor Moshnin, and he was born in 1759, the youngest of three children. Tall and strong, gifted as a carpenter and filled with a passion for life, Prokhor seemingly "wasted" his life by choosing to become a monk at the age of eighteen. He was renamed Seraphim, or "fiery one," after the fierce angels around God's throne (see Isaiah 6:2). Inspired by the Bible and the desert fathers, he moved into the woods to live as a hermit, devoting himself to Scripture, prayer, repentance, and spiritual combat.

In this "farther hermitage," as he called it, his life exuded a Christlike compassion and gentleness. Eyewitnesses reported animals, even a lumbering black bear, eating out of Seraphim's hands. On one occasion, he was beaten by three robbers and left for dead. When the authorities captured them, Seraphim forgave the thugs, proclaiming that when we refuse to forgive "it is as if a rock settles on the heart."

Later in his life, at the Spirit's prompting, he threw open the door of his hermitage. Visitors came streaming into his secluded cabin. Suddenly the contemplative hermit developed a bustling ministry of counseling, prayer, and healing. Couples with troubled marriages came to him, and after Seraphim spoke barely a word, their marriages were reconciled. He became a spiritual father to thousands, addressing each person as "my joy" and blessing them with "Christ is risen!" He challenged people, "Acquire a peaceful spirit, and thousands around you will be saved."

My Pilgrimage as a Hermit

Fueled by the stories of Saint Seraphim and the desert fathers, I decided to try an abbreviated version of the hermit lifestyle. About ten years ago, I attempted a twenty-four-hour retreat at *Pacem in Terris* (Latin for "Peace on earth"), a Franciscan retreat center nestled on 220 acres of pristine woods in central Minnesota. *Pacem* was my first choice because their brochure called their small prayer cabins "hermitages" and I would be a "hermit." So for twenty-four hours, much like the holy fool Saint Seraphim of Sarov, I would live like a hermit, without running water, a phone, a television, a computer, mail, or even the soft hum of a refrigerator. Only God, me, and the dark silence of birch trees and wild prairie grass.

Ah, the bliss of my hermitage! Much to my surprise, I really liked the hermit lifestyle . . . for about forty-five minutes. After reading a psalm, eating some bread and cheese, and taking a nap, I still had more than twenty-three hours left. I panicked. What would I do for the next twenty-three hours? Against the explicit instructions of my spiritual director, I converted my hermitage into a backwoods office. I read books and journals (mostly on prayer, of course), outlined my next sermon series, fretted over the oil leak in my minivan, and kicked myself for not doing something useful and productive.

I struggled to live as a hermit for a day; how did Seraphim do this for thirty years? And what was the point of his retreat into uselessness? Why would anyone, especially a vibrant and gifted young man like Saint Seraphim, withdraw into the woods to spend years praying, memorizing Scripture, and combating the forces of darkness? Why didn't the holy fools do something useful—like renewing the church, feeding the hungry, spending the entire weekend driving kids to soccer games, or building another strip mall? With all the pressing needs around us, isn't the hermitage experience at best a waste of time and at worst a form of narcissistic escapism?

The One Thing We Need

To begin with, I started learning what the holy fools did *not* mean by the contemplative life. These hermitage-dwelling holy fools were emphatic that contemplation could not coexist with self-ishness. The twentieth-century spiritual writer Thomas Merton blasted phony contemplatives who flee into the "false sweet-ness of narcissistic seclusion."[1] Focusing on achieving personal "fulfillment" or having a "spiritual experience" strangles true contemplation.

I also discovered that a truly contemplative life never justifies unloving escapism. As I witnessed in the life of Saint Seraphim, a Christ-centered hermitage experience will, over the course of a lifetime, make me more interested and more concerned for the world's brokenness. True contemplative prayer doesn't blind us to the needs of the world; instead, it transforms our entire vision of the world. I noticed over and over again that, with a Christ-imbued vision of the world, these holy fools entered their hermitage only to reemerge and then reengage the world with pure deeds of mercy and witness. The Christ life poured out through their words, their actions, and their very presence.

So what is the essence of the contemplative life? What did the holy fools like Saint Seraphim and the desert fathers hope to find on their trek into the woods or the deserts? Once again, it was a small, quiet Bible story (a particular favorite of holy fools) about marginal people that helped me understand true contemplation.

In the tenth chapter of Luke's Gospel (verses 38-42), Jesus and his friends are "*on their way*" when they descend on a woman named Martha. This tiny story contains the epitome of holy folly: surprise, subversion, even humor. Martha, we are told, "*welcomed him into her home*," presumably with open arms (we're not sure if she was equally excited to greet Jesus' entourage of sweaty, socially inept, fish-reeking traveling companions). Not to worry, though, the ever-efficient and cheerful Martha, the maestro of hospitality, the get-it-done woman of excellence, begins preparing an elaborate feast for the small mob.

While Martha is busy setting the table, she notices her younger sister, Mary, sitting quietly at the feet of Jesus. Jesus is teaching, and Mary, the true holy fool in this story, hangs on every word. Her face, her heart, her hands—everything about her is focused and intent. Meanwhile, Martha churns with resentment. As she continues her efficient, dutiful service, perhaps she considers just bringing out a tray of bread so she can listen to Jesus. But Martha is "distracted," the text tells us. Uncentered and agitated, Martha spins and wobbles like a washing machine with an unbalanced load.

A while later, Martha enters the room with a tray of food, the fruit of her efficient labor, only to find Mary still listening to Jesus. Finally, Martha erupts and proceeds to issue a direct order to Jesus: "Lord . . . tell her to come and help me." This is a shocking and disrespectful way to treat Jesus, but notice that the path of anticontemplation eventually leads to manipulation. Rather than contemplate, we will try to manipulate our circumstances, other people, and even the Lord himself.

If I didn't know the story so well I'd expect Jesus to side with Martha. "Martha, Martha, Martha," he should say, "you are so right. Mary, you can contemplate later. For now, let's all practice servanthood by helping your sister." Instead, Jesus subverts our normal expectations by rebuking Martha: *"You are worried and upset over all these details."* Imagine that! Martha is doing all the work. She's the efficient, dutiful, busy one, but Jesus commends the holy fool Mary. Then he gently chides Martha, *"There is only one thing worth being concerned about."* Mary has chosen that "one thing," and Jesus promises, *"It will not be taken away from her."*

Mary was contemplating. That is the "one thing" we need, Jesus said. Mary wasn't striving to be a contemplative. She just sat at Jesus' feet, paying attention to his words and lingering in his presence. She simply abided in Jesus and drew life from him (see John 15:1-5). In one sense, she chose to be utterly useless, unproductive, and unbusy. But Jesus subverts our expectations by declaring that Mary was pleasing God because she was doing the "one thing" required.

Contemplation involves a lifestyle of not just thinking about God or doing things for God. It is a life of being *with* God, sitting *with* Jesus, receiving from Jesus until we overflow with his grace and truth. It doesn't bypass our intellect or the necessity of activity; it simply focuses everything we do and think into a union of being with God.

When I was fifteen years old, my family planned a trip to the north shore of Lake Superior. Midway up the shore there is a little town called Schroeder, Minnesota, a rustic town with a string of cabins near the Cross River. After winding its way through the Superior National Forest, the Cross River finishes its course with a furious waterfall that flows into Lake Superior. Before our family vacation, we studied pictures of the Cross River and the awesome waterfall. We looked at postcards and listened to stories. But when we finally took the trip, I'll never forget the experience of actually sitting in the Cross River. On a hot July afternoon the fierce waterfalls pummeled my body, spraying into my face, cooling my sunburned shoulders.

For me, that is a picture of contemplation. True contemplatives don't just look at pictures of God and acquire information about God; they yearn to experience God firsthand, to be sprayed by the waterfall of God's grace and truth and holiness. The psalmist commanded us to "taste and see that the LORD is good" (Psalm 34:8). Contemplation involves "tasting" God. Jesus told us to "come to me and drink" (John 7:37, NIV). Contemplation means "drinking in" Jesus. Jesus also told us to "abide" in him (see John 15:4-5, NKJV). Contemplation is abiding in Jesus, drawing life from him.

Seraphim trekked into the Russian forest and the desert fathers traveled into the forbidding solitude of the Nile desert region because they weren't satisfied with just looking at pictures of God or acquiring knowledge about God. They wanted to taste and drink God until he overflowed into the world around them.

Of course, a true Christian contemplative remains grounded in the concept of God's initiating grace, which simply means that God is always the driving force behind our contemplation. In other words, God wants us much more than we want him. God is always seeking us before we ever seek him. According to the larger story of the Bible, all of us are on a spiritual journey—but apart from God's grace, it's always a journey *away* from God. The brilliant young philosopher Simone Weil rejected the term "seeker" after God. "I may say," she wrote emphatically, "that never at any moment in my life have I 'sought for God.' For this reason . . . I do not like this expression, and it strikes me as false."[2] Our contemplative quest begins with the God of grace, who seeks, woos, stirs, and draws us—sometimes kicking and cursing—into his Kingdom of love and delight. But apart from God's initiating grace, human contemplatives wouldn't exist.

The Danger of Pragma

In my initial encounter with the holy fools, this all sounded dreadfully abstract, impractical, and unrealistic. What does it mean to "be with God" and "waste time with Jesus"? And isn't it just plain wrong to strive to be "useless, unproductive, and unbusy"? Certainly, there is a balance between contemplation and action, but I started to grasp the prophetic edge to the holy fools' lifestyle. Most of us have been completely captured by a Martha-like spirit of activism. The contemplative spirit of Mary or Seraphim may seem appealing, but down deep our lives are dangerously distracted, being pulled and yanked and agitated by many things.

Part of this Martha-like busyness is external. We live in a distracted culture. "Western culture is so powerful and alluring," contends author Ronald Rolheiser, "that it often swallows us whole. . . . The hardest thing to sustain within our lives today is [contemplative] prayer. Everything militates against it."[3] Most of us are committed to the dogma and practice of pragmatism. The term itself comes from the Greek word *pragma*, or business, but it also implies Martha-like efficiency, productivity, and busyness. As I read about the holy fools, I started to notice that pragmatism is really the underlying ethos in our culture, government, schools, and most of our churches. As a result, most of us are noncontemplatives or even anticontemplatives. Deep in our hearts we are driven and controlled by two fundamentally pragmatic assumptions: (1) Worth lies in achievement. You are good and worthy because you produce and achieve. (2) Doing counts for everything; being counts for nothing. "Being," whatever that means, is impractical, inefficient, unproductive, and worthless. Of course, the problem with this pragmatic outlook is that major areas of life—prayer, worship, rest, celebration, parenting, friendship, and love in general—are notoriously nonpragmatic. You can't reduce God or the spiritual life or a marriage or a friendship to five easy steps for instant success.

But another manifestation of our "Martha syndrome" is internal. We have distracted hearts. Rolheiser calls it "unbridled restlessness." In our age, restlessness has become a raging fever. If you don't believe me, try this experiment. Ask people, "How are you?" and then note the number of people who respond with one word: "Busy." Busyness or unbridled restlessness has become the defining mark of our culture. Our lives (and our children's lives) must move at hyperspeed. We want to experience everything that life has to offer—and we want it right now! There is no time to think or rest or breathe deeply. It's as if the entire point of our existence as creatures designed to glorify God and live passionately for him and with him for all eternity implodes into the black hole of staying busy.

This is the spirit of Martha: busy, efficient, productive, restless, and greedy for new experiences. We are Martha. As a result, the contemplative faculties—those spiritual muscles that should allow us to pay attention to God, to dwell with God, to taste God—begin to atrophy.[4]

A Hunger for the Hermitage

We're quick to label Seraphim an unproductive escapist. Why didn't he do something really "useful," like chop down trees, cover the land with concrete, and erect an evangelistic theme park? But then again, what would the holy fools say about us? I imagine Seraphim of Sarov gazing into my eyes, shouting out, "My joy!" and then gently reprimanding, "Look at your life: You are a constant blur of activities and distractions. You sit down to pray and everything swirls in a fog. You can't focus and pay attention. You have twenty-seven Bibles in sixteen different translations, but the word of Christ does not fill your life (see Colossians 3:16). God draws near to you, but your heart remains far from God. So rather than bring the peace of Christ into your activities and relationships, you merely bring your fractured, frantic, hyperdriven, overextended life into everything you do. Is that what you call 'fruitful ministry'?"

I am starting to realize that I desperately need Seraphim-like holy folly. My mentors, the holy fools, challenge my assumptions and subvert my unquestioned commitment to pragmatism and unbridled restlessness, exposing my spiritual sickness and deadness.

As I begin to understand the purpose behind a holy fool like Seraphim, it awakens in my heart a hunger for the hermitage, a desire for the contemplative quest. Naturally, my first question is, How do I do it? How do I practice contemplative prayer? Unfortunately, that is a highly pragmatic question. It is a question a Martha might ask. "Give me a technique," I demand. "A neat, logical series of steps so I can master and control contemplative prayer."

Unfortunately, I am also discovering how steps and techniques work along the contemplative way:

Step 1: Steps kill contemplative prayer.

Steps 2–100: See step 1.

A tidy step-by-step process fits my pragmatic bent, but those much more experienced on the contemplative path warn me that the demand for steps often suffocates the spirit of contemplation. Nor is contemplative prayer focused on the goal of accomplishing something or having a "spiritual experience." The apostle Paul warned us that we don't even know how to pray as we ought (see Romans 8:26). I am slowly learning that contemplative prayer begins not with competence and mastery but with a willingness to face my helplessness. True contemplatives embrace the reality of spiritual poverty (see Matthew 5:3). They remain beginners for the rest of their lives.

I still keep the following prayer of Thomas Merton's close by my Bible. It's a reminder that the path to contemplative prayer begins by admitting I'm lost:

> My Lord God, I have no idea where I am going. I do not know the road ahead of me. . . . Nor do I really know myself, and the fact that I think I am following you does not mean that I am actually doing so. But I believe that the desire to please does in fact please you. I hope that I will never do anything apart from that desire. And I know if I do this, you will lead me by the right road. Therefore, I will trust you always though I seem to be lost and in the shadow of death. I will not fear, for you are ever with me.[5]

A Simple Journey into Contemplation

Even though there are no magic steps to follow, I still need some kind of "handles" or "movements" to guide me in the journey of contemplative prayer. The holy fools did want to be helpful. They tried to shock us and jolt us out of complacency, but they never intended to leave us frustrated and hopeless. So although they never arranged a neat, simple list of steps to manage and master contemplative prayer, they did provide some handles. So how do we begin the journey into contemplative prayer, the practice of being with Jesus?

Perhaps a concrete picture will help clarify the handles or the movements of contemplative prayer. Let's say that at 11:00 p.m. I finally arrive at home after a grueling day and a draining three-hour committee meeting. As I enter the hallway, I realize that I never edited my son's paper on the solar system and nobody organized the twenty-one pairs of shoes in our front hallway, and in my aggravation I snap at my wife before she falls asleep. Like Martha, I am distracted by many things.

But I have the dubious privilege of surpassing Martha with a secret weapon of distractibility—I own a remote, so I can channel surf. So as I sit in a comfortable chair with the remote nestled in my right hand, I watch Jerry Seinfeld dump his girlfriend because she separates her peas and eats them one at a time. Then I surf to the *Letterman* show, where "Betty" performs a "stupid human trick" by snorting milk up her nose and then shooting it out her tear duct. (This actually happened!) Before I head to the kitchen to snort some milk through my nose, I flip to an infomercial, where Jim explains how a hair transplant revived his sagging self-esteem.

I turn off the television, but by now a bunch of monkey-thoughts have invaded my heart, screeching and swinging from branches in my tangled neurons, pelting me with mental bananas. They are out of control, and I'm seriously distracted and agitated. So I walk into the kitchen, make a cup of hot tea, sit in my chair (without the remote), and grab the last thing I want right now—my Bible. My body shrieks with internal noise, but as I hold the hot tea in my hand, allowing it to steam and steep, it suddenly occurs to me that the house is quiet. All day long a vicious conspiracy of noise has inundated me. The silence feels strange but good and even sweet.

My mind continues to churn, but I am starting to feel the leather Bible cover in my hands and the movement of my lungs as

I breathe. I smell the cinnamon in my hot tea. It strikes me that although I've talked about God and done things for God today, I haven't remained with God. And then the thought occurs to me: God is here and I am in his presence. God has been seeking me. This is infinitely better than Betty's stupid human trick and Jim's hair restoration.

I open my Bible (not at random—actually, I've been working my way through the Psalms in order) to Psalm 63. In the deep silence of the midnight hour, I read verse 1: "O God, you are my God; I earnestly search for you. My soul thirsts for you; my whole body longs for you." Then I stop. *Yes,* my heart says, *that is so true.* I am so thirsty for God. I want God more than anything. Slowly, lovingly, I say the words again: "My soul thirsts for you; my whole body longs for you." I repeat those words perhaps twelve to fifteen times until they begin to penetrate my defenses and distractions.

Then I start praying, "God, forgive me. I am thirsty for you." What else can I say? The thirst is so palpable that I cannot "advance" to another prayer. It's like a deep groan welling up from the depths of my stomach. I can only respond to the thirst by praying, "Lord, Jesus, have mercy on me, a sinner." So I pray those simple prayers over and over again.

And then I'm quiet again, only this time it is a deeper, richer, Christ-filled silence. Eventually, I will edit my son's paper, apologize to my wife, and organize the shoes, but for now, like Mary, I choose to be unproductive, lingering in Christ's presence. Unlike the pragmatic world I live in, there is nothing to accomplish. I don't demand an emotional experience or a "touch from God." I am actually more aware than ever of my spiritual darkness, emptiness, poverty, and deep longing for God. But like an empty cup, I sit under the waterfall of his presence, from his fullness receiving "grace upon grace" (John 1:16, NASB). God is here. The seeking God. The questing God. The triune God of grace fills the room and now fills my heart.

That is one picture of contemplative prayer. Obviously, we contemplate best when we set aside a day or perhaps even a week to be with God. But we can also live contemplatively by making small choices throughout the day to dwell with God.

I can't spend thirty years in the forest, but after a hectic Tuesday I can turn off the television, enter the silence, read a psalm, or sit silently with Jesus for thirty minutes. Little by little, I start to think and pray and live like a holy fool.

The Journey into the Hermitage

If we analyzed this experience (*analyze* literally means "to pull apart"), we'd discover certain handles or movements to contemplative prayer: silence, recollection, meditation, and rest. These are not steps or techniques, but they are spiritual disciplines that guide us in our quest to "taste and see that the Lord is good" (Psalm 34:8).

Silence: Finding a Quiet Place

Prior to my pathetic dip into contemplative prayer, all the books and experts kept telling me that I needed more silence. Actually, they said that contemplative prayer is impossible without silence and solitude. The prophet Habakkuk reminded me that "the LORD is in his holy Temple. [Therefore] let all the earth be silent before him" (Habakkuk 2:20). Jesus himself often escaped into an "isolated place" so he could pray (Mark 1:35). Mother Teresa echoed this idea by saying that "God is the friend of silence."

I tried silence . . . and I found it excruciating.

I live in a noise-saturated world, and I also have a noisy

heart. The holy fools warned me that this internal noise erects the biggest barrier to contemplative prayer. As soon as I sit down to pray, as soon as I slip into a quiet place, the outside noise stops but my internal noise kicks into high gear—whirring, sputtering, clicking, and sometimes screeching like a broken engine that won't shut down.[6]

Contemplatives resist this addiction to noise by finding a place for silence and solitude. It may be at midnight in your living room. It may be at noon on a bench under an apple tree. It may be at three o'clock in the afternoon as you shut your office door for fifteen minutes. The holy fools were nudging me toward a clear decision: Carve out a time and a place to escape the bombardment of noise. Capture a few "scattered crumbs" of silence and solitude. But they also warn me: You'll have to fight for it. In most instances, it won't just happen. On the front end, silence requires discipline and vigilance.

Recollection: Gathering the Scattered Pieces of Your Heart

If we regularly enter silence and refuse to run away, it will slowly give way to a sense of recollection. Recollection, an essential forerunner to contemplative prayer, is the polar opposite of Martha's distraction. In the act of recollection, we begin to gather the scattered pieces of our hearts and bring them into focus. In biblical language we obey God's advice to "be still, and know that I am God!" (Psalm 46:10). In Jesus' words we come to our senses (see Luke 15:17) and journey back to the Father's house. Recollection isn't an attempt to deny our thoughts—even bad thoughts. It's merely an attempt to gather them up, honestly face them, and then offer them to God in joyful self-forgetfulness. We simply rest in God's presence and start to pay attention.

I started a very simple practice of recollection by writing the following words in my journal: "Lord, it is Monday at 7:00 a.m., and I'm on my front porch swing sipping coffee. Here I am, Lord." This simple act initiates recollection. My mind, my heart, and even my body can stop and acknowledge where I am and what I'm doing. I am sipping coffee. It is Monday morning. And most important, I am in the presence of the Lord, the holy and loving God of the universe. My mind stops racing. My restless and noisy heart begins to settle into God. I am re-collecting myself.

Meditation: Attending to God's Word

Recollection isn't an end in itself; it leads to meditation. For the desert fathers and other holy fools, meditation was always meditation on Scripture. Psalm 1 extols the blessed person who meditates day and night on the Word of God. The holy fools practiced this attentive, persistent rumination on Scripture.

In the discipline of study we read and analyze; we understand the background and context of a certain portion of Scripture.[7] But in the act of prayer-filled meditation we ponder the words we have studied. It is sustained and focused thinking on a specific portion of the Bible. Notice I said *portion* and not *text*. A text is something you study. A portion, like a portion of double-layer chocolate cake, is something you savor. Meditation involves slowly ingesting, tasting, savoring, experiencing, and focusing on God's Word. And it involves the entire being—lips (as we pray and meditate out loud), mind, imagination, and will.

Let's say, for instance, that I choose a simple portion of Scripture: "God is our refuge and strength, always ready to help in times of trouble" (Psalm 46:1). I could study the text, analyzing the structure of Hebrew poetry, cross-referencing this verse with similar verses, outlining the entire psalm, and so on. But for now I will focus on the portion right before me. With simple and loving attention, I read and then say the words out loud (thus involving my physical body in the action). Then, as I read it and say it again, the Spirit pierces my heart with a verse or a word. I slowly begin to repeat the words of Scripture—lovingly, attentively. I say the words over and over again, attending to each word, allowing the truths to seep into my mind and heart. As they sink into my being, I start to make connections with my life. Yes, I have troubles right now. As a matter of fact, I'm almost always in some "times of trouble." But in the midst of these troubles, God is my refuge and strength. Yes, I do need strength. But God is my strength! As we attend to God's Word, it gradually becomes a part of our very being.

Rest: Dwelling in God's Love

Then we rest in God's love. Our hearts open and listen. Without forcing an "experience of God," we simply acknowledge our poverty and weakness. We can't control the technique to force a certain result. We can only wait and rest; God will give us exactly what we need. Like Mary, our only "job" is to sit at his feet and wait. For the contemplative life is "not so much a way to find God as a way of resting in the God whom we have found, who loves us, who is near to us, who comes to draw us to himself."[8]

Recently my friend Jill discovered the essence of contemplative prayer. In the context of her desire to maintain perspective in the grueling and highly pragmatic world of academia, Jill "stumbled" into contemplative prayer. "My quiet times are different now," wrote this brilliant PhD student. "I used to be only rigorous about my devotional life—reading one chapter in Proverbs, one chapter in the New Testament, applying the verses, and then dutifully completing my prayer list. Now I balance this rigor by also reading just a few verses at a time. Then I sit there and literally bask in God's presence and love for me. I feel like Jesus has been saying to me, 'I love you.' I've heard about God's love so much that it has become a cliché. But to hear his voice, in the depths of my heart, saying he loves me . . . how can I not keep perspective? How can I avoid the intent gaze of someone who's so passionately in love with me like this?"

The Fruit of Contemplative Prayer

Is this life of contemplation worth the time and effort? Jesus thought so. He even said that without the deep experience of abiding in him, our lives would be like dry and barren branches that are ready to be burned (see John 15:6). But the contemplative life brims with fruitfulness (see John 15:5).

Consider the story of Seraphim of Sarov. "What's so special about Seraphim?" we might ask today. "So the guy spent thirty years in the forest. He could have done something useful for God. How does that challenge me today?"

But a true holy fool might say, "Look at his life. By the time he opened the door to his hermitage, the grace of Jesus poured through every action and every word he spoke. His heart was so steeped in the waterfall of God's grace that he overflowed with the healing presence of Jesus. And people really experienced Christ's healing. The healing wasn't in a program or a strategic plan. Jesus' presence simply poured out of this man until his words and even his smile brought healing to broken lives. Out of all the words you've spoken and the plans you've made, how many times have you brought someone right into the healing presence of Jesus?"[9]

Such is the power of the subversive holy fools for Christ. They take the surprising, comical, countercultural path of trekking to their hermitage only to reemerge with compassion and the healing power of Jesus.

QUESTIONS FOR REFLECTION

On a scale of 1 to 10, what is the level of distraction and noise and busyness in your life? What do you like and dislike about your present level of busyness?

"Deep in our hearts we are driven by two fundamentally pragmatic assumptions: (1) Worth lies in achievement. You are good and worthy because you produce and achieve. (2) Doing counts for everything; being counts for nothing." How do these two assumptions play out in your life and in our culture?

Read Luke 10:38-42. Based on this story, how does Mary exhibit a contemplative spirit? How can you apply this to your life today?

If Seraphim of Sarov observed your life over the course of the past week, what do you think he'd say? Would there be any areas in which he'd challenge you to change your course?

Of the four "handles" of contemplative prayer (silence, recollection, meditation, and rest), which is the hardest for you to practice? What can you do to make at least one of these handles more a part of your life?

CHAPTER 8

Practicing Secret Goodness

If you put wax in front of a fire it melts; and if you pour vain praises on the soul it goes soft and weak in seeking goodness.

A treasure that is known is quickly spent: and even so any virtue that is commented on and made a public show of is destroyed.

ABBA SYNCLETICA

A FEW YEARS AGO I heard an old Jewish tale entitled "If Not Higher." The story opens by describing a small village's beloved rabbi who disappeared every Friday morning. Unable to find him anywhere, the devoted villagers boasted that their rabbi must ascend to heaven every Friday so he could talk with God.

One day, however, a newcomer to their small village heard the stories and merely scoffed. "People don't ascend to heaven. I'll tell you where your rabbi really goes on Friday mornings."

So the next Friday morning the newcomer crept into the woods by the rabbi's house. He quietly watched the rabbi rise, say his prayers, and much to the onlooker's surprise, dress in the clothes of a common peasant. The rabbi walked into the woods, chopped down a small tree, and then cut it into firewood. Still following at a safe distance, the newcomer saw the rabbi carry a bundle of wood to a shack in the poorest section of the village. An old woman and her sick son gladly received the bundle of wood for the coming week. They thanked the anonymous woodsman, unaware that it was the rabbi in disguise.

Deeply moved by the rabbi's secret goodness, the newcomer became his disciple. And whenever he heard the villagers say, "On Friday mornings our rabbi ascends all the way to heaven," the newcomer would quietly add, "If not higher."

This story of hidden goodness illustrates a key aspect of the lifestyle of Christian holy fools. Like the rabbi, holy fools often lived lives of secret spirituality. The beauty of holiness was hidden behind the disguise of folly.

In a way, the holy fools' spirituality of secret goodness was sheer slapstick. They lived like stately princes whose true faces were hidden behind ridiculous masks. During the day these holy fools wandered the streets and alleys, frequenting inns and bars, consorting with the dregs of society, acting like complete moral buffoons and spiritual bunglers,[1] shocking and irritating the righteous. At night they would then withdraw to their secret hiding places, perhaps a stable or a hut on the margins of the city, where they could remove their bungler's masks, sink to their knees, and begin their evening of unbroken and passionate prayer.[2] People who spied on these holy fools when they were in prayer claimed that they were standing on holy ground.

Stories abound about the intentionally hidden goodness of holy fools. After returning from a long season of solitude in the desert, the Russian holy fool Symeon was apprehensive of spiritual honors and public acclamation for his spiritual prowess, so he prayed that "all his works might remain hidden." Just to be safe, Symeon began his ministry by climbing into the pulpit and pelting nice church ladies with nuts. Later, as his popularity grew, he kept up the disguise by feigning mental illness and laughing with his "girlfriends" (i.e., prostitutes). Although those tactics aren't necessarily ones we'd choose to imitate, we also need to take the danger of "Christian celebrity" as seriously as Symeon did. In private, however, Symeon withdrew to secret places, known only to his closest friend, where he petitioned God to shower his life and the world with mercy.[3]

A pair of holy fools, Theophilus and Maria, children of affluent parents from the city of Antioch, also perfected the art of secret goodness. Dressed in outrageous costumes—Theophilus as a mime actor and Maria as a prostitute—this pair of holy fools entered the city and acted like buffoons, performing a comedy in the street, poking fun at the lukewarm village priests. The narrator of their story, however, a historian named John of Ephesus, followed them to their hiding place at the city's outskirts. Peering over a city wall, John records that he watched Theophilus and Maria "take off their masks" and shine with inner holiness. "I saw that both . . . stretched out their arms to heaven in prayer in the form of a cross, and after a time they fell upon their faces in prayer, and they stood up and again fell on their faces in prayer . . . and they went through the same form for a long time."[4]

Some of the holiest desert fathers sought other creative ways to avoid human applause for their spirituality, perfecting a secret, stealthlike approach to the spiritual life. In one story, a wealthy judge traveled into the desert seeking the famous Abba Moses, asking the first person he met where he could find this incredible holy man. "Don't waste your time," the desert dweller replied, "Abba Moses is a heretic and a fraud. He's not any of the things people say that he is." When the judge returned to the city, he told people about the "real" Abba Moses—a fraud and a heretic. "Wait a minute," a friend inquired, "by any chance was the desert dweller a tall black man?" "Why, yes," replied the judge. "Ah," his friend said, "that was Abba Moses himself. You met the man at his best. He'd never make anything of his own sanctity."

On another occasion, whenever people journeyed to praise a holy man named Abba Simon, he would slip into his unholy disguise. As Simon stuffed himself with bread and cheese or climbed a tree and polished its branches, the celebrity seekers would look with disgust at the glutton and idiot and then continue searching for the saintly Abba Simon.[5]

Choosing the Little Way

Once again, I encounter the strange antics of the holy fool, and again they strike me as strange and excessive. I don't want to imitate every detail of their lives, but then again, I am starting to see that they offer a perspective I need to gain—and a correction I need to hear. "Don't do anything with a view to being praised by others," urged the early desert father Cassian. That seems reasonable, but aren't these examples extreme? Why would anyone intentionally hide their spirituality? If you're holy and you know it, why not just show it? Come now, pelting fine church ladies with nuts, dressing up as a mime, climbing trees and polishing branches? What's the point of that? Why did these people labor to perfect the fine art of hidden goodness?

First of all, I am starting to understand the clear and compelling vision that drove the holy fools' behavior. They were passionate about following Jesus, listening to his words and his life, and then imitating him without compromise. Of course, I can't slavishly copy Jesus in every detail of my life—otherwise I'd have to move to Palestine and become a thirty-year-old single Jewish man wandering the countryside as an itinerant preacher. Dallas Willard provides a helpful guideline in the quest to follow Jesus: "[As a disciple] I am learning from Jesus to live *my* life if he were I. I am not necessarily learning to do everything he did, but I am learning how to do everything in the manner that he did."[6] At its heart, the imitation of Jesus involves emulating the spirit of Jesus more than copying every single detail of his life.

But I also notice that the holy fools never took this as a license to refine the ragged edges of Jesus' teachings. In Matthew chapter 6 Jesus warned about the dangers of what we could label "theatrical righteousness." According to Jesus, there's a name for people who perform good deeds "to be admired by others"—they're called hypocrites. They treat the world as their personal stage—primping, preening, puffing, and performing with all their might. Spirituality becomes the arena to garner the praise of others, rather than the altar to offer ourselves to God.

With the help of the holy fools, I am starting to pay more attention to Jesus' clear teaching on this subject. On one occasion (see Matthew 6:1-18), Jesus painted a ridiculous caricature of this insatiable quest for praise and attention.

> When you give to someone in need, don't do as the hypocrites do—blowing trumpets in the synagogues and streets to call attention to their acts of charity! I tell you the truth, they have

received all the reward they will ever get. But when you give to someone in need, don't let your left hand know what your right hand is doing. Give your gifts in private, and your Father, who sees everything, will reward you.

When you pray, don't be like the hypocrites who love to pray publicly on street corners and in the synagogues where everyone can see them. I tell you the truth, that is all the reward they will ever get. But when you pray, go away by yourself, shut the door behind you, and pray to your Father in private. Then your Father, who sees everything, will reward you. . . .

And when you fast, don't make it obvious, as the hypocrites do, for they try to look miserable and disheveled so people will admire them for their fasting. I tell you the truth, that is the only reward they will ever get. But when you fast, comb your hair and wash your face. Then no one will notice that you are fasting, except your Father, who knows what you do in private. And your Father, who sees everything, will reward you.

As usual, Jesus' insights are so timely and relevant for us. Most of these showy religious folks can be found hanging around churches today—and sometimes I find the same person inside my heart. "Hey, do you think you could inscribe my name on that gold plaque for the new children's wing?" asks Betty, a high-profile contributor. Then there's Ted, the self-appointed "prayer warrior," who dominates the public airways with his tortuously long-winded prayers. And finally there's George, the guy who looks like he has a permanent case of mononucleosis. "Well, actually, I'm not sick," he gasps and wheezes, "but I have been fasting for three weeks and I can barely stand."

Frankly, I'm much smoother than Ted, Betty, and George, but inside my heart I know that God often detects a seething brew of spiritual pride and insecurity: *If people only knew how dedicated and selfless I am—how much I pray, serve, love, give, sacrifice—if they were only aware of how much I know about Scripture and spiritual disciplines, if they only knew how much my ministry is growing, they would certainly be impressed. At the very least, they would pay attention, pat me on the back, encourage me, and reward me.*

In their typical shocking style, the holy fools bring me back to the sharp-edged and countercultural teachings of Jesus. Quit being a hypocrite. Close your closet door and pray to your Father, who is unseen. Let your good deeds and your spiritual disciplines remain so quiet, so secretive, so hidden that your left hand doesn't even know what your right hand is doing. This is the stealth approach to spirituality: It's undetected because you intentionally fly under everyone's radar—even your own. The entire spiritual life becomes a conspiracy of hidden and quiet kindness, goodness, discipline, and light. On three occasions in this passage Jesus told us that God the Father delights to reward this secret goodness (verses 4, 6, and 18).

Of course, the holy fools based their faith not just on Jesus' words; they also realized how much of his life was hidden and secret. How did he enter the world? Quietly, humbly, and secretly. The King of kings was disguised as the child of a peasant; he was a carpenter and a slave (see Mark 6:3; Philippians 2:6-8). Throughout his ministry, Jesus often repelled the adulation of the crowds, warning stunned miracle watchers to say nothing (see Mark 1:41-45).

Because they embraced the countercultural lifestyle of Jesus, holy fools pursued a life of secret goodness. One such holy fool, Saint Therese of Lisieux, a nineteenth-century French nun, called this hidden spirituality "the Little Way." In the Little Way, Therese sought the joy of being ordinary, simple, and even unnoticed. She knew that one of the greatest dangers in the spiritual life is the desire to be known as holy, gifted, or "spiritually mature."

According to Therese, our conversations about our ministries and our walk with God are often mingled with a great deal of self-love and a demand for praise from others.

The solution is to follow the Little Way by ignoring our good deeds, putting our eyes on Jesus, following in his footsteps, and eschewing the lure of theatrical righteousness. On one occasion, a young nun complained to Therese that it was exhausting to serve God. Therese asked her how it felt when others complimented her. "I feel so revived," the novice nun said. "It sounds like it's not the work that's causing you fatigue," replied Therese, "but your need to have your work recognized."[7] Holy fools are revived by the fact that God notices and rewards secret goodness.

Starving Our Inner Narcissist

Naturally, this is easier said than done. I've fought the lure of theatrical righteousness throughout my life. By the time I was thirteen years old, for instance, I had won seven Olympic gold medals. And even more astonishing, I was the most valuable player on the U.S. men's basketball team. Unfortunately, all these miraculous achievements occurred on the driveway of my parents' home in suburban Minneapolis. Thousands of imaginary fans used to watch me play—and they were never disappointed. Inevitably, as the clock wound down, I would calmly sink two free throws, steal the inbounds pass, and, weaving between five much taller Russian defenders, shoot an off-balance jumper at the buzzer for a U.S. victory.

Thirty years later, I'm slightly comforted by the fact that I wasn't alone in my little fantasy world. Psychologist David Elkind claims this experience, known as the "imaginary audience," is common to most adolescents in our culture. According to Elkind, "Teenagers feel that they are always on stage and that everyone around them is as aware of, and as concerned about, their appearance and behavior as they are themselves."[8]

Fortunately, we grow out of it . . . or do we?

Although the intensity may diminish, in some ways the imaginary audience seems to hound us for life. In its extreme form, we can even develop what psychologists call a narcissistic personality disorder, a needy quest to have everything in the world revolve around self. It is the neediness that constantly demands and whines, "Look at me. Let's focus on my needs. Notice my achievements. Aren't I a good boy? Am I spiritual or what? Hey, I did something good; now give me applause, an award, a prize, a raise, or a bonus."

According to the Greek myth, Narcissus was a young man of physical perfection and unparalleled beauty. One day as he knelt to drink at a crystal clear pool, he saw a lovely face reflecting back at him. Of course, it was his own face, but Narcissus fell in love. Losing all desire for food or drink, Narcissus continued his loving gaze at his own reflection until he died a lonely, tragic death. It's no coincidence that some of our most alert social observers have dubbed our age the "culture of narcissism."[9]

I'm sad to say that most of us possess a cluster of Narcissus-like tendencies. In Martin Luther's words, everyone's sinful self remains *incurvatus in se,* curved in upon itself in self-preoccupation. Similarly, the Russian saint Theophan the Recluse compared the unredeemed self to a long, thin shaving of wood that hopelessly and continuously curves inward on itself. Doctors, diesel mechanics, counselors, university students, college professors, receptionists, church volunteers, pastors—this quest for attention is no respecter of persons. We all clamor to be center stage. And, Jesus and the holy fools warn us, nowhere is this pull more powerful than in the spiritual life. So our good deeds, our work for God, our ministries, and our spiritual disciplines—the very things that should "uncurve" us and open us to God's presence—sometimes curve us in a tighter circle around our hollow selves.

Garrison Keillor once said that there are only two ways to cure "raging narcissism": Have children or move to a foreign country where people don't care who you are or what you do. Jesus and the holy fools offer a third and, I believe, more effective strategy: Starve the inner narcissist by forgetting ourselves and focusing on God.

How do we do this? By perfecting the art of secret goodness. As much as possible, the holy fools instruct us, hide your good deeds. Don't promote your own goodness or spiritual progress. As we say on Long Island, "Forget about it." Like the small village's beloved Jewish rabbi, it's better to disguise yourself as a lumberjack than attract a round of applause for your humility. It's better to be a clown, a buffoon, a pathetic street mime, a glutton, or a tree-polishing freak than it is to be a spiritual celebrity. It's better to keep your good deeds secret than it is to advertise them (or even to allow others to do the advertising for you). By keeping their goodness quiet, hidden, and secret, holy fools begin to shift attention and praise to where it truly belongs: God.

My wife often reminds me how a tough little Holocaust survivor named Corrie ten Boom handled her status as a "Christian celebrity." After telling her story of redemption, crowds of people would throng to shower her with praise. Corrie used to say that she imagined herself receiving long-stem roses from every well-wisher. Then when the crowds left, she imagined taking all the roses she had received and offering the whole bunch to Jesus.

Did the holy fools take things too far? Of course they did—that's the point. They startle and awaken us to our raging self-centeredness, the pride that curves even our spiritual disciplines back in upon ourselves. When we're self-centered, when we practice theatrical righteousness, "the ego is bloated and the soul shrivels."[10] By perfecting the art of secret goodness, we reverse the process: The ego shrivels and the soul revives.

Finding True Spiritual Freedom

Holy fools believed that this conspiracy of secret goodness is the only path to spiritual freedom. Theatrical righteousness (*look at me, notice me, pay attention to me*) leads to bondage. When the applause doesn't come, or when others give it sporadically or imperfectly, how do we respond? At our best, we're disappointed. At our worst, we demand it. Perhaps the good deeds will grow louder and more noticeable. And if the praise does not come, we begin to walk through life with a deep, churning resentment: *Why don't you notice me? Why don't you meet my needs? Why don't I receive the recognition I so clearly deserve?*

Theatrical righteousness doesn't just lead to resentment; it also creates confusion. There are so many voices to heed, so many people to please. For example, I recently listened to someone tell me, "No offense, Pastor, but your sermons are shallow and I'm not being fed." Later that afternoon, an engaged couple left my office hugging me and declaring, "You are the greatest man and the greatest preacher we've ever met." Who am I? Am I an ineffective, pathetic excuse for a disciple of Jesus? Or am I a hero, possibly the next inductee to the Ministry Hall of Fame?

Whoever I am, if I'm focused on my image or my status as a "godly man," it's certainly confusing. The conflicting expectations of others will almost always lead to confusion and exhaustion. Our lives become a frantic race—panting, running, sweating—to please the crowd of people in our lives. Real relationships with God and others become impossible because we can't rest, we can't stop.

Resentment, confusion, exhaustion—surely there must be a better way. And there is: Jesus' way of holy folly leads us into spiritual freedom. That's why the holy fools recommended the liberating power of what they called *apatheia,* or indifference. This does not imply an indifference to feelings (although at times it is interpreted that way); it means learning to ignore unimportant matters so we can jettison every bag that isn't essential for the spiritual journey. One of the bags we must leave behind is our compulsive and needy demand to have our egos stroked by others. The desert fathers told a story that speaks to apatheia. A young brother, seeking advice on how to become holy, was instructed by an older monk named Macarius to visit a cemetery. On his first visit, he was instructed to mock the dead, shouting insults and throwing stones.

"What did they say to you?" asked Macarius.

"Nothing," said the younger monk.

"Good, now go back and praise the dead, shouting compliments and showering them with praises."

Once more, the young man obeyed the strange advice.

"What did they say?" asked Macarius.

"They still didn't say anything," he replied.

"Ah, they must be holy indeed," Macarius concluded. "You insulted them and they did not reply. You praised them and they did not speak. Go and do likewise, my friend, taking no account of either the scorn of men or their praises."

Again, apatheia is not the inability to feel; it's the ability to focus on God rather than the applause or the criticism of others. We can certainly learn from the criticism of others. We can also give thanks to God for the encouragement of others. Both can be good gifts from our Father's loving hand.

But holy folly is slowly teaching me that I don't have to crave praise and flee criticism. I can learn to release the bulky luggage of human praise. My heart becomes lighter and I begin to fly toward God.

Of course, we all still have an entirely legitimate need to be praised. When my three boys were younger, I could never sit beside a pool without constantly hearing, "Dad, watch this. Watch this awesome cannonball dive—AHHHHHHH! Watch me swim from one end of the pool to the other end. Watch us play catch." I realized that watching and then praising is a compulsory parental duty and delight. We watch and praise. We just do it—instinctively and attentively. And I'm no different than my children. I need affirmation and appreciation and (dare I say) applause. Okay, I'll admit it: I still crave praise.

Commenting on the legitimate hunger for praise, C. S. Lewis wrote, "Pleasure in being praised is not pride. The child who is patted on the back for doing a lesson well, the woman whose beauty is praised by her lover, the saved soul to whom Christ says, 'Well done,' are pleased and ought to be. For here the pleasure lies not in what you are but in the fact that you have pleased someone you wanted (and rightly wanted) to please." But according to Lewis, the trouble comes when we move from "I have pleased him" to "What a fine person I must be to have done it." We aren't delighting in the praise of another anymore; we're just delighting in ourselves.[11]

So the question for my life is not whether or not I will have an audience; the holy fools just make me ask the question of which audience I will choose. And they want to deliver me—with shock tactics if need be—from the tedious burden of courting the wrong audience.

A Stealth Approach to the Spiritual Life

How do we practice a lifestyle of secret goodness, a stealth approach to the spiritual life? First, the holy fools gently encourage me to track and confess the pervasiveness of my self-centeredness. Self-centeredness can be so deeply rooted that even a lifestyle of secret goodness can promote spiritual pride, so those more mature in the faith instruct us to be brutally honest about our self-centeredness. I started keeping a prayer journal so I could record every time my heart acted like the thin shaving of wood curved inward on my spiritual performance. Did I demand that others notice me for my good deeds in order to revive my spirit? I could note it, confess it, and then let go of it.

Second, I am learning that the only way to release my raging self-centeredness and self-promotion and self-defensiveness is to stand in the righteousness of Christ. If I truly believe in the Cross of Christ, if I truly believe that he died the death I should have died and lived the life I should have lived—for me and on my behalf—so I could receive his perfect track record of righteous living, then God will praise me right now. This astounds me. I thought I knew the gospel, but now I am beginning to appropriate the practical power of the gospel. It is almost too good to be true: I have the righteousness of Christ. I please God the Father as much as Jesus (God the Son) pleases the Father. So, "if God is for us, who can ever be against us?" (Romans 8:31).

The holy fools are also teaching me to measure spiritual achievements by God's scale, not my warped scale. I realize that I often crave a spirituality of the loud, the big, the famous, and the flashy. By contrast, Jesus and the holy fools typically preferred a spirituality of the quiet, the small, the obscure, and the simple. When God is our audience, our best acts are often a beautiful secret between him and us.

A while ago I breezed into a crowd to deliver the weekly sermon. It was a good deed—and a very public one. Many people shook my hand, expressing gratitude for the "lovely" message. Then, after fulfilling my duty, I scooted toward the back door, but on my way out I passed three severely arthritic women who were gingerly holding watermelon slices in their gnarled fingers. They motioned me to come over. "Would you like to join us for a little watermelon?" they asked hopefully. I hesitated at the door. "I suppose I could stay for a moment." Thirty minutes later we were still sharing stories and munching on watermelon slices. The crowd was gone; it was just God, three elderly women, and me.

As usual, I measured the importance of these two scenarios by the size of the crowds: hundreds versus three. But part of living as Jesus' disciple is learning to see that both scenarios had the same audience: God. He doesn't count human applause or earthly recognition. Instead, he rewards the hidden deeds, the unseen motives, the quiet acts of mercy and love.

Third, we can rest in Therese's Little Way, the contentment of being ordinary, unnoticed, and hidden. Francis de Sales, a spiritual director from the 1600s, once cautioned, "Great opportunities to serve God rarely present themselves but little ones are frequent." So he urged all believers to "practice those little, humble virtues which grow like flowers at the foot of the cross: helping the poor, visiting the sick, and taking care of your family." In this way, we can "direct all our actions, no matter how lowly they may be, to the service of Divine Majesty."[12]

My friend Jim is learning to find contentment in this little way of secret goodness. As an emergency room doctor, Jim's work is sometimes stressful and downright gruesome. Twelve-hour shifts grind down his body and mind. Yet, unlike many of his colleagues, Jim's work is rarely noticed or applauded. He just does the best he can to patch up severely broken people. Who could blame Jim for grumbling and resenting his job? But last year, while participating in a Lenten stations of the cross service, Jim had a profound encounter with Christ. He saw what Christ had suffered for our salvation—the "foolishness of the cross." He recalled how that suffering did not receive praise or admiration. And then Jim sensed God quietly say, "Jim, you have a cross to bear too. Do your job faithfully for me without human applause, and I will reward you. Follow me with a life of secret goodness."

Jim's patients and his church family may never know that something shifted in Jim's soul. They may never applaud or even notice. But perhaps they may notice a little more contentment and a little less resentment. Why? Because every time Jim sews stitches or sets a broken bone, he's not just doing it for his patients. He's doing it for Christ. And that brings great joy and freedom. Such is the spirit of a contemporary holy fool, an artist perfecting small acts of secret goodness for Jesus' sake.

REFLECTION QUESTIONS

How does Christian subculture promote the quasi worship of Christian celebrities? How is this healthy? unhealthy?

Read Matthew 6:1-18. What does theatrical righteousness look like? What does Jesus say about secret goodness?

Do you need to have your work recognized by others? When does that cross over into theatrical righteousness?

How is the "inner narcissist" alive and well in your heart?

C. S. Lewis said, "Pleasure in being praised is not pride."
What's the difference between our legitimate hunger for
praise and our tendency to just delight in ourselves?

Where do you sense Jesus calling you to practice secret goodness in your life?

AWAKENING TO A LIFE
OF SPIRITUAL PASSION

CHAPTER 9

Living in Joyful Surrender

The fool in Christ is likewise free, because he has nothing to lose. . . . He cannot be exploited, for he has no ambition; and he fears God alone.

KALLISTOS WARE

WHEN I WAS A SENIOR in high school, our posh suburban mega-church sponsored a monthlong missions conference. Every week I'd listen in rapt attention as the speakers regaled us with gut-wrenching tales about orphans living on the streets of Manila, scrounging through garbage cans and fending off rats, or believers in the Soviet Union gathering underground and trying to outwit KGB double agents. The stories made my blood run hot.

And then every week the speakers would issue their passionate but predictable ultimatum: "Surrender your whole life to Jesus. The days are short and Jesus is coming back soon. Don't hold anything back because God despises your lukewarm commitments. So surrender everything *right now!*" And then, just as predictably, we'd sing all four verses of hymn #399, "I Surrender All."

Of course, I wanted to surrender everything. If someone had given me a ticket to Manila or Moscow, I would have ditched my shallow, suburban existence and devoted my entire life to feeding the orphans or helping my oppressed brethren. But then, within forty-eight hours of leaving the missions conference, my heartfelt surrender would unravel. My mom would tell me to clean my room and I'd blatantly ignore her. After hearing about the orphans in Manila, what's an unkempt suburban bedroom? I not only refused to honor my father and mother, but in that forty-eight-hour binge of antisurrender, I'd manage to break four or five other commandments as well. Apparently my most sincere attempts at surrender didn't stick. I felt like a defective Christian and a spiritual loser. To paraphrase Flannery O'Connor, I'd never be a saint, but maybe I could be a martyr if someone surprised me and killed me quick.

For years I looked for a biblical loophole for the surrendered life. Although I publicly prayed gutsy prayers like "Send me anywhere, Lord," my real prayers were often timid gripes such as "God, can't you cut me some slack?" But after reading the Bible for more than thirty years, I haven't found any slack. Actually, the New Testament seems to tighten the call for complete surrender. "For [Christ's] sake I have discarded everything else," claimed Paul, "counting it all as garbage, so that I could gain Christ" (Philippians 3:8). In another place Paul pleaded with us to surrender and "give your bodies to God because of all he has done for you. Let them be a living and holy sacrifice" (Romans 12:1).

Jesus didn't cut us much slack when he said, "If any of you wants to be my follower, you must turn from your selfish ways, take up your cross daily, and follow me" (Luke 9:23).

It was along these lines that C. S. Lewis concluded his masterpiece *Mere Christianity*, with a stirring summons to a surrendered life:

> Keep nothing back. Nothing that you have not given away will ever be really yours. Nothing in you that has not died will ever be raised from the dead. Look for yourself, and you will find in the long run only hatred, loneliness, despair, rage, ruin, and decay. But look for Christ and you will find Him, and with Him everything else.[1]

Lewis identified the key themes of surrender. First, it involves a release, a letting go of everything, placing it in God's hands. It means telling God, "Father, here it is: my one and only life with so much passion and possibility. I give it to you today—all my gifts, my hurts, my time, my work, my energy, my relationships, my sex life, my body. I hold nothing back. You gave it to me in the first place, so I offer it all back to you." It really is an all-or-nothing bargain. Second, as Lewis observed, surrender leads to joy, not misery. A nonsurrendered life or a halfsurrendered life in the end leads to rage and ruin and decay. Surrender, in contrast, unleashes joy and passion.

Reckless Abandon

Honestly, the all-or-nothing aspect of surrender, holding nothing back, giving it all for Jesus, made me feel squeamish. Whenever we sang "I Surrender All," I felt like a complete fraud. How can anyone do that? How is it possible to surrender *everything*? The idea of total surrender terrified me. What kind of God would demand that? And if I did surrender, what would God do with me? So I always held back, offering God my halfhearted, compromised, mediocre version of surrender. For years I wondered if there were really people who could take up their cross daily and give their bodies to God. But then I met the holy fools. I couldn't comprehend how they did it, but the holy fools actually followed Lewis's advice to "keep nothing back," living with a joyful and carefree surrender before God.

For instance, Saint Francis of Assisi managed to forsake his father's massive wealth, sell everything, strip off his clothes, and walk into the woods.[2] Eventually he did put clothes back on and, among other things, kissed lepers, rebuilt the church, sang songs, founded a band of world-changing troubadours, challenged the pope, preached to a sultan, and endured unbelievable suffering. Then there was Patrick. After Celtic warlords kidnapped Patrick and forced him to feed pigs for six years, he escaped and returned to his homeland, England. He started living a safe and predictable life until God spoke to him in a dream and told him to go back to Ireland. Patrick surrendered to God and plunged his life into the people who had imprisoned him. The Russian holy fool Nicolas exhibited his joyful surrender to God by confronting Ivan the Terrible. Sticking a bloody steak in Ivan's face, Nicolas said, "You see this bloody steak? That's how you treat your people." For some reason, Ivan, who definitely had a penchant for head-chopping activities, let Nicolas live. Damien was another holy fool who surrendered his life to God. He volunteered to leave the safety of his ministry and move to the godforsaken island of Molokai, where the Hawaiian government was exiling all the lepers, treating them as criminals and sentencing them to die on Molokai. But Damien joyfully spent the rest of his life there, loving lepers and eventually becoming a leper. All these holy fools actually pulled it off; they surrendered everything.

And the holy fools didn't just grit their teeth and surrender. They did it joyfully. They lived with reckless abandon, just like the woman who anointed Jesus before the crucifixion (see Matthew 26:6-13). It's another classic holy folly story: A marginal, "foolish" person—an unnamed woman, no less—surprises and subverts the respectable spirituality of her day. She sneaks in under the radar (women didn't just barge in on a dinner party like this) carrying a bottle of costly perfume. Many scholars assume the alabaster jar, perhaps a family heirloom, contained a rare type of pure nard imported from India. As she breaks the jar open and the aroma wafts through the air, she pours the precious liquid on Jesus' head. Pure, rare, precious—her devotion is just like the nard, an act of joyful surrender.

She's my mentor in holy folly. I tend to be much more like the disciples. They gripe and gossip like cranky old men at a small-town diner: "What a waste! This perfume could have been sold at a high price and the money given to the poor." Although they never venture out with passionate faith, they're experts at critiquing others who do risk it all. Under perfect circumstances, maybe, just maybe, they'd use an eyedropper and carefully squeeze out one drop of the precious liquid. But the whole bottle? How shocking! How inappropriate and wasteful!

I also think about my friends "George and Brenda Smith," veteran Bible translators in the remote mountains of an Asian island. (Because George and Brenda work in a remote and hostile environment, I won't use their real names.) Back in 1959, as I was sucking on my baby bottle, they were busy setting up chairs in their living room for the church that I now pastor. A few years later, they felt the tug from God to translate the Bible into a previously unwritten language, which has been their job description for the past forty years. After George polishes up Ezekiel, the entire Bible will be available in this as-yet unwritten language. George and Brenda continually amaze me because they're so radical, surrendered, and poured out—and so normal and kind. They aren't wild-eyed, judgmental fanatics. But in spite of forty-plus years of tedious work, diseases, discouragement, loneliness, and constant death threats, they've persevered with a quiet passion and a joyful surrender.

A Jolt to Our Mediocrity

I'd like to say that these stories of surrender thrilled my soul. Instead, on one level, they just made me feel like a spiritual slug. In contrast to these poured-out, radical holy fools, my life looked so mediocre and blah and unsurrendered. They were spiritual Tabasco sauce, spicy and lively and red-hot. I was a can of Campbell's cream of mushroom soup, a glob of smooth but utterly bland, gray spirituality. Looking at their spiritual lives, the depth of their surrender, I felt uncomfortable.

Of course, in one sense, that's the point of holy folly. Such a passionate approach to the spiritual life is *supposed* to shock my system and jolt me out of mediocrity. The holy fools' lifestyle of joyful surrender shouldn't leave me defeated and guilty, but it should challenge and stir and unsettle my soul. On the spiritual journey I don't just need comfort; I also need a kick in the rear.

Few people understood this aspect of holy folly better than the philosopher Søren Kierkegaard.

> The greatest danger to Christianity is . . . not heresies, heterodoxies, not atheists, not profane secularism—no, but the kind of orthodoxy which is cordial drivel, mediocrity served up sweet.

> . . . Christianity does not oppose debauchery and uncontrollable passions as much as it opposes this flat mediocrity, this nause-ating atmosphere, this homey, civil togetherness, where admit-tedly great crimes, wild excesses, and powerful aberrations cannot easily occur—but where God's unconditional demand has even greater difficulty accomplishing what it requires: the majestic obedience of submission.[3]

The holy fools refused to settle for the "cordial drivel" and "mediocrity served up sweet" that often passes for Christian spiri-tuality. Kierkegaard helped me realize that my spiritual medioc-rity, my halfhearted surrender to God, needs a jolt every once in a while. A spiritual jolt is a natural response to what the Bible calls holiness, the sense of goodness and purity and "otherness" that comes streaming from the beauty and uniqueness of God.

According to the apostle Peter, whenever we encounter the holiness of God the Father it should unsettle our souls, causing us to "live in reverent fear of him" (1 Peter 1:17). The holiness of God produces a shock to our systems, a jolt of healthy fear.

In the same way, as I encounter the stories of my mentors, the holy fools, I allow them to stretch and unsettle my spiritual life. These men and women really did offer their bodies and their lives to God as living sacrifices. And they did it over and over again, with utter joy and delight and carefree abandon. It is per-fectly appropriate to let them challenge my mediocrity, even if I feel uncomfortable.

The Long Search for Surrender

This awareness didn't resolve the practical problem of total sur-render—as in, how do you do it? The New Testament called for surrender ("Give your bodies to God . . . a living and holy sacrifice" [Romans 12:1]). C. S. Lewis echoed it ("keep nothing back"). And the holy fools actually lived it. They challenged my mediocrity. They showed me my lack of surrender. They proved that joyful surrender is possible, but they didn't help solve the problem of my unsurrendered life. So I embarked on a long search. How can I exude the joy of surrender—the delight in resting fully in Jesus, obeying him, and encountering his holiness so that I become holy?

First of all, I noticed (with a sigh of relief) that, just like me, the holy fools often lurched and lunged forward on their journey toward full surrender. When I was seventeen, I thought I could deliver myself to God in one neat little package with glittering paper and a shimmering gold bow. Now that I'm in my late forties, more often than not I'm still scrambling to attach scraps to cover my messy gift box for God. I latched on to the analogy used by author Anne Lamott to describe famous writers:

> People tend to look at successful writers . . . and think that they sit down at their desks . . . feeling great about who they are and how much talent they have and what a great story they have to tell; that they take in a few deep breaths, push back their sleeves, roll their necks a few times . . . and dive in, typing fully formed passages as fast as a court reporter. But this is just the fantasy of the uninitiated. I know some very great writers . . . and not one of them writes elegant first drafts.[4]

I see the same principle at work in the holy fools. None of them created an elegant spiritual life on their "first draft." That is a "fantasy of the uninitiated." So, although I allow the stories of the holy fools to challenge and stir me, they don't need to crush or demoralize my spirit. Recklessly abandoning myself to God will remain a lifelong struggle. As a matter of fact, it's *the* struggle of my Christian life.

But another thing I am discovering, to my utter amazement, is an unlikely ally and mentor in surrender: Jesus, the ultimate holy fool. Jesus didn't just tell me to surrender; he actually lived a life of joyful surrender. I discovered Jesus' lifestyle of surrender by accident as I read the Passion story on Good Friday. It's really an ironic story. On the one hand, Simon Peter, a man who should surrender, never does. In spite of Jesus' clear warning ("I tell you the truth, Peter—this very night, before the rooster crows, you will deny three times that you even know me" [Matthew 26:34]), Peter keeps insisting, "I got it, I got it. I can handle it without you, Lord. I don't need to surrender." But then Jesus, the one I always assumed lived beyond the realm of surrender, actually surrendered to God the Father. As he prays at Gethsemane, he cries out, in effect, "Let it be as you will, not as I will. I surrender my life to you" (see Matthew 26:39).

Jesus surrenders? Does God need to surrender to God? If that's true, if God the Son really does surrender to God the Father, then that tells me something profound about my life. Surrendering to God isn't some otherworldly or even "spiritual" act. Surrender is just life—life the way it's supposed to be lived. Surrender constantly flows in God's Trinitarian life. The Son surrenders to the Father. The Father seeks to honor the Son. The Spirit surrenders by pointing back to both the Father and the Son. The Father and the Son send the Spirit as their representative. Surrender is woven into the life of God and into the fabric of the universe. Surrender is the most natural, normal posture for the human soul.

This is crucial for me because it means I can no longer view surrender as a threatening appeal or a once-and-for-all ultimatum. For most of my spiritual life I've acted like Harrison Ford's character in the movie *The Fugitive*. He plays a successful heart surgeon named Dr. Richard Kimble, who is wrongly accused of murdering his wife and sentenced to death. After Dr. Kimble escapes from a prison bus, an obsessed U.S. marshal played by Tommy Lee Jones hunts him like a wild animal. Jones is utterly unrelenting, but Harrison Ford stays one step ahead of him. In one tense scene, Jones confronts Ford and tells him, "You're surrounded and there's no way out. Put your hands up, get on your knees, and give up." I'm convinced that's how most people view surrendering to God. God appears with his cosmic bullhorn and life-confining handcuffs and demands that we give up. So with our heads hanging in shame and defeat or maybe even anger and defiance, we wave our white flag to God and give up. But that's not the way Jesus demonstrated a life of joyful surrender.

Surrender Flows from Love

Jesus revealed a Father who certainly isn't a U.S. marshal hunting us down. He doesn't even tell us to surrender until he shows us how to surrender. By his actions Jesus says, "When it comes to surrender, you can never say, 'I got it.' You can't do this on your own. You'll never surrender unless you watch me do it and then live in me so I can do it in you."

And how did Jesus surrender? For Jesus, surrender always flowed from love, not fear or threats or attempts to try harder. I noticed that Jesus' entire view of surrender hinged on two words in his Gethsemane prayer: "My Father." In those two words, Jesus radically redefined the religious quest for all people. God is not some cosmic sheriff hunting us down and forcing us to submit. Nor is God some vague force of goodness or beauty. God is our Abba, our Father. *Abba* is a word from Jesus' mother tongue of Aramaic that means "daddy" or "papa." It's an intensely personal and intimate address for God—so intimate that most people of Jesus' day would be aghast to use such boldness and familiarity with God. Amazingly, the early church retained this word as a way for all who are in Christ to address God (see Romans 8:15).

True surrender is never just a response to fear; it's a response to love. Should we fear God? Yes, God is awesome and holy and just—and we aren't. But real and lasting surrender is fueled by love. Notice Jesus. He isn't afraid of his Father; he loves his Father. The Father doesn't destroy the Son; the Father loves the Son.

For Jesus, love—not guilt, pressure, threats, or manipulation—is the best motivation for a life of joyful surrender. I have a friend named Larry who works for a wonderful ministry called Long Island Youth Mentoring. In a recent newsletter Larry told the story of visiting a group of teenage boys in jail. On his first several visits to these young men, they were angry and defensive. Their faces stayed contorted as if they were preparing to spit. "What are you doing here?" they hissed. "What's in it for you?" But as Larry continued to visit, gently displaying unconditional love to the boys, their defenses slowly melted and they opened their hearts. Larry summarized the experience with this maxim about surrender: "People will only be real when they feel safe. People will give you their hearts when they feel loved and embraced." God knows that. So the gospel, the Good News about Jesus, tells us how sinful, hostile people can feel safe before a holy God. There is nothing to hide because God knows it all, Jesus died to forgive it all, and the Spirit lives within you to reveal it all.

An Authentic Spiritual Quest

The struggle of surrender propels us into the heart of a gospel-centered quest. The religion-centered quest comes in many different forms, but in one way or another it tells me, "If I obey, if I perform, if I can do it well enough, if I'm born into the right family . . . I will be accepted before God." It's mainly up to me; the pressure is on me. If I surrender and maintain my surrendered state, if I keep jumping through the right hoops, God will embrace me. But according to a biblical interpretation, religion always leads to two disastrous alternatives: self-righteousness (because I have performed and I am good enough) or guilt and anxiety (because I'm not sure if I've measured up to the rules).

In sharp contrast, a gospel-centered spiritual quest turns all of that upside down by saying, "No, because I am already loved by God in and through Jesus Christ, I will obey and surrender my life." The gospel isn't just a different religion; it spells the end of religion and the beginning of new life. The gospel states that I'm the worst sinner on the planet because I know how deceptive *my* own heart can be. As a result, the gospel concludes that total surrender—living for God with my whole heart—really is impossible . . . unless Christ lives in me and for me. So an authentic gospel-centered quest keeps driving me back to Jesus and his unfathomable grace.

I'll never forget a raw young Christian named George who attended the first church I pastored. George came from a severely broken home, and his own past included years of alcoholism. He constantly struggled to grasp the basics of the Christian life. When I preached a sermon on surrendering our lives to Christ, George bellowed, "That's impossible. How do you surrender everything?" When I spoke about loving our enemies, he was incensed. "Are you kidding? I can't forgive all these people. This is too much."

When I talked about God's grace being available to anyone, George accosted me at the door, refused to shake my hand, and yelled, "This Jesus stuff is just plain crazy! It's too hard." I told him not to be discouraged. I said, "I think your anger and bewilderment are good signs. They mean you finally understand that living for Jesus really is impossible—unless Jesus lives in and through you. That's the key, George. It's Christ in you and his grace for you."

Pursuing a gospel-centered spiritual quest melts our sin-frozen hearts, unleashing a river of love, wonder, and gratitude. When we grasp the gospel, when Christ lives in us and through us with his righteousness and power, we want to live for him. We want our lives to turn into joyful worship and our joyful worship to turn into wonder-filled surrender.

The gospel tells us that God has lavished us with grace because he wanted to; it gave him pleasure to pour grace all over us (see Ephesians 1:5, 9). Like the woman anointing Jesus, God took the pure nard of his own life and poured it all out on the cross. Gospel-centered holy fools allow this lavish grace to seize their hearts, imaginations, and wills. This grace leads naturally into wild praise and joyful surrender.

In this regard, my friend Willis certainly qualifies as a gospel-centered holy fool. Willis worked long, hard hours fixing furnaces, driving fuel oil trucks on frigid Minnesota nights, and gathering hay bales on muggy summer nights until the mosquitoes descended. But Willis always exuded a God-sized love and a deep astonishment that Christ saved him, forgave him, and lavished him with grace. It didn't matter what we sang during worship services, Willis almost always cried. But I think he cried the hardest during the third verse of "How Great Thou Art": *"And when I think that God, His Son not sparing / Sent Him to die, I scarce can take it in / That on the cross, my burden gladly bearing / He bled and died to take away my sin."* By the time we started to sing the chorus, Willis was choking back the tears. At that point, Willis wasn't trying harder to love God; God's grace had already pierced his heart, and the clear, cool liquid of love was flowing out of the very center of his being.

The Ordinary Fruit of Surrender

A gospel-centered spiritual quest unleashes wonder, worship, love, gratitude, trust, and joyful surrender. The quest of religion just makes us insecure or self-righteous. Only the gospel can convince us to surrender. It's the beautiful logic of being loved beyond all reason.

And surrender always produces fruit. It's earthy and practical. It's never just for us, for our cozy, private but utterly narcissistic spiritual feelings. Jesus' surrendered life was, first of all, for his Father, but it was also for our sakes. His surrender blessed us. In the same way, our surrender will blossom, grow, and ripen in order to bless the world.

Sometimes our surrender blesses the world in big, dramatic ways. When my friend Joel surrendered his life to Jesus, he started visiting Cambodia with a Christ-based ministry that rescues young girls and boys who are trapped in the global sex trade. This ministry intervenes by setting up safe houses where these children can find freedom, faith in a loving heavenly Father, cleansing from their feelings of shame and guilt, protection, housing, education, and training. Another friend, Delbert, surrendered everything to God and then sold his successful printing business in Florida. He moved to Zambia to work with the poorest of the poor. Now he spends most of his time designing and manufacturing small hand-cranked carts for people who can't walk and who can't afford wheelchairs.

I'd like to see God do something big and dramatic with my surrender. I also believe that our globally connected world means that we can and should allow our surrender to make an impact on worldwide issues such as slavery and spiritual darkness and poverty and cruelty. But then again, God also wants me to surrender the "little things" in my life—the ordinary areas of living that produce ordinary fruit. This also flows from a gospel-centered spirituality.

In the New Testament, the spiritual act of surrender always flows naturally into the ordinary, concrete, and unspectacular but fruitful realms of life. For instance, when Paul said, "You died to this life, and your real life is hidden with Christ in God" (Colossians 3:3), such a concept could float untethered into the ozone of our spiritual lives. But then Paul planted it firmly in everyday life by saying, "Whatever you do or say, do it as a representative of the Lord Jesus, giving thanks through him to God the Father" (Colossians 3:17). Once again, surrender is imminently practical, earthy, all-encompassing, and fruitful for others.

This earthbound side of surrender should have an enormous impact on the way we live our lives. Surrender isn't just an emotional response to an intense experience such as a monthlong church missions conference. Surrender involves our whole lives. Somehow many of us have adopted the idea that God is only pleased—or at least more pleased—with what we might call "religious activities." The assumption behind this view is that there is a split, a gap, a chasm between two realities: the important sacred realm and the inferior secular realm. Unfortunately, that means that a huge chunk of our lives has been severed from God's good purposes for us. We only allow surrender to affect a small slice of who we are and what we do.

But according to the Bible, God didn't invent the sacred/secular split. We did. In the Bible, our joyful surrender affects everything we do—mowing the lawn, eating chili, taking the dog for a walk, meeting a friend for coffee, driving kids to soccer practice, taking a nap, attending worship services, writing a check for world missions, and of course, working a job for twenty to seventy hours a week. According to the Bible, whatever we do or say should be done "as a representative of the Lord Jesus, giving thanks through him to God the Father." Surrender cuts through every area of our lives—except sin. According to the biblical story, your whole life matters to God. Your whole life is charged with glory and purpose and goodness. Your whole life is charged with significance as a joy-filled surrender to serve God and love your neighbor.

In a tender story from the desert holy fools, a dying abba named Paphnutius asked God to show him his equal upon the earth. Much to his surprise, Paphnutius's "spiritual twin" was not another monk; instead, it was a former thief turned street musician and leader in a local village. Paphnutius urged his protégés that "no one in this world ought to be despised . . . for in every condition in human life there are souls that please God and have their hidden deeds wherein He takes delight; whence it is plain that it is not so much profession or habit that is pleasing to God as the sincerity and affection of the soul and honesty of deed."[5]

The English poet Gerard Manley Hopkins advocated an all-encompassing, earthy view of surrendering our lives to God:

> It is not only prayer that gives God glory but work. Smiting on an anvil, sawing a beam, white-washing a wall, driving horses, sweeping, scouring, everything gives God some glory if being in His grace you do it as your duty. To go to communion worthily gives God great glory, but to take food in thankfulness and temperance gives Him glory too. To lift up the hands in prayer gives

God glory, but a man with a dungfork in his hand, a woman with a slop pail, give him glory, too. God is so great that all things give Him glory if you mean that they should.[6]

In other words, there are no sacred/secular distinctions. Every legitimate vocation and activity becomes an opportunity to tell God, "Father, I surrender this to you." For instance, my friend Greg sometimes attends Sunday morning services with grease and oil on his hands because he has been up half the night fixing furnaces. Is that a high and holy calling? Well, on a cold night in New York, who else is going to fix your furnace? Every time I see Greg with those grease-streaked hands, I feel like I am standing on holy ground.

My friend Bob is a biochemistry professor and world-renowned expert on complex carbohydrates. One afternoon I sat in his college classroom at Stony Brook University and listened as Bob gave a lecture to his first-year biochemistry students. Listening to Bob describe the amazing interactions between amino acids and lipids and proteins, I wanted to shout, "This is astounding! Someone has to tell other people about this. Someone needs to declare the miracle of life." Then I realized that's why Bob is at Stony Brook University.

Even our hobbies are part of this seamless act of total surrender. While I was reading through the Bible, I found a wonderful little phrase tucked into 2 Chronicles, of all places. Chapter 26 describes the "secular" achievements of King Uzziah. As the author recounts the practical and earthy fruit of Uzziah's surrender to God (the surrender is mentioned in verses 4-5), he adds a wonderful phrase in verse 10—Uzziah "loved the soil." It doesn't say he loved the soil because it served a spiritual purpose. Based on a straightforward reading of the text, I get the sense that he loved it just because he loved it. It's like someone who likes fishing or doing needlepoint or playing soccer or composing a jazz piece or making a soufflé just because it's good. For Uzziah, soil was fun and challenging and interesting for its own sake. In other words, Uzziah's joyful surrender to God even transformed the way he looked at dirt.

All of life becomes an act of worship and an opportunity to serve and please God.

I love the way Eugene Peterson describes Romans 12:1 as a call to a life-affirming, fruit-producing act of total surrender. "Here's what I want you to do, God helping you: Take your everyday, ordinary life—your sleeping, eating, going-to-work, and walking-around life—and place it before God as an offering" (*The Message*). That's the spirit of holy folly. God showers us with mercy and grace. As our hearts are seized by this grace and mercy, we respond by joyfully surrendering our lives back to him.

The Freedom of the Holy Fool

As I continue on the path with Jesus, as I focus more and more on the goodness of a God who is for us, as I imbibe his poured-out love for me, surrender seems natural. It happens slowly, quietly, but I suddenly realize that I've surrendered more than I ever thought possible. As I begin to let go and surrender, as I relinquish and pour back to God, I taste the startling spiritual morsel that the holy fools feasted on every day: spiritual freedom. That's the true secret of every holy fool. Fools for Christ—the poured-out people, the surrendered people—have nothing to lose. You can't scare them. You can't exploit them. You can't bully them. You can't buy them. They are already sold out.

When my son visited the National Gallery in London, he described to me the painting of the sixteenth-century Dutch painter Gerrit van Honthorst called *Christ before the High Priest.* More than any other picture I know, this painting captures the essence of the holy fool's spiritual freedom. The high priest, visibly angry and hostile, sits at a table, shaking a long finger at Jesus, sentencing him to death. As a single candle shines on Jesus, we marvel as he stares, intently and lovingly, at his accuser. With his hands tied and his robe torn, Jesus is surrounded by smug, angry witnesses. He owns nothing, and yet the face of Jesus draws us in to his deep strength and gentleness. Accused and condemned, Christ is still focused and centered.

This is perfect freedom. Jesus is free from hate, from fear, from exploitation, from trying to please anyone except his Father in heaven. And in his grace, he invites us to step into that freedom as well. Such is the power and the beauty of joyful surrender. Such is the glory of holy folly.

QUESTIONS FOR REFLECTION

How do you respond to the idea of surrendering all to Jesus? Does it make you excited, fearful, or shame-filled—or a combination of all three? How have you struggled with surrender throughout your life?

Read the story of the holy fool in Matthew 26:6-13. How does this woman exhibit joyful surrender? In what ways are you like her (or do you want to be like her)? In what ways are you like the disciples in this story?

Kierkegaard said, "The greatest danger to Christianity is . . . not heresies, heterodoxies, not atheists, not profane secularism—no, but the kind of orthodoxy which is cordial drivel, mediocrity served up sweet." In what ways are you (or we) battling this danger of spiritual mediocrity?

In what ways are you lurching and lunging forward in your search for full surrender?

How does Jesus' example of surrender help us to surrender? How does the gospel—knowing that we are loved and accepted in Christ—free us to live lives of full surrender?

What is one practical, earthy area of your life that God is nudging you to surrender to him?

CHAPTER 10

Walking with Discernment

Many of our most cherished plans for the glory of God are only inordinate passion in disguise.

THOMAS MERTON

Some wear out their bodies by fasting, but because they have no discretion, this only puts them further away from God.

ANTONY OF EGYPT

TWO YEARS INTO MY first pastorate, during the muggy days of a Minnesota August, a sweaty stranger walked into our tight-knit community of 460 people. The stranger, a healthy young man in his midtwenties, breezed into town "on a mission from God."

The mission consisted of dragging an eight-foot, one-hundred-pound cross from Seattle to New York City. "But I'm telling the truth, Pastor," he solemnly whispered. "God told me to do it." And apparently God selected us to serve as his halfway refueling spot. Our cross-lugging evangelist just wanted food, a warm bed for a week, a daily shower, a chance to talk to the local newspaper, some cash to finance the second half of the trip, and a "few minutes" in the pulpit. We gave him everything he needed, although I did draw the line at the pulpit time. So after the worship service, while the rest of us "normal" Christians drank coffee and ate doughnuts on the church lawn, the stranger hoisted the massive cross on his shoulder, and with a nod and a "Thank you kindly, folks," he headed toward New York City.

Who was he? Did the stranger really have a mission from God? Did God actually speak to him and tell him to drag an eight-foot cross from coast to coast? Was he a holy fool or an unholy fraud? On the one hand, he struck me as a lunatic. He probably would have had to kill me or threaten my family before I gave him five seconds in the pulpit. On the other hand, what if he really was a holy fool? How would we know the difference?

As strange as my encounter with the cross-bearing man was, it wasn't an isolated incident. We all know people (and have probably been the people) who start a conversation with the three scariest words in religious conversations: "God told me . . ." Those words send shivers up the spine. "God told me to do this. God told me that you have a demon. God told me to marry you. God told me to become a pro basketball player. God told our country to attack your country. Because I'm an 'artist,' God told me to ramble incoherently for twelve minutes while I introduce this next song."

Obviously, the spiritual path is littered with great ideas, projects, assumptions, and missions that supposedly came from God but really just came from our own disordered hearts. "Many of our most cherished plans for the glory of God," warned Thomas Merton, "are only inordinate passion in disguise."[1] In other words, our most sincere "God told me" might be a slick cover for "I told myself."

Of course, people really do hear from God. For instance, I'm fully convinced that God told Francis of Assisi to kiss a leper and that God told Hudson Taylor to grow a pigtail and go to China. On some level, I'd like to think that God told me to write this book. So how do we tell the difference between holy folly and just plain stupidity, emotional immaturity, or even worse, spiritual con artistry and outright lunacy?

Finding Balance

The early desert holy fools weren't impressed with mere spiritual activity. According to one story, three young men came to an experienced hermit and one by one shared their impressive spiritual achievements.

"I memorized the entire Bible," boasted the first young man.

Unimpressed, the hermit replied, "And you have filled the air with words."

"I wrote out the entire Bible by hand," claimed the second protégé.

But the hermit calmly said, "And you have filled the window ledge with manuscripts."

The third young man excitedly said, "Well, there is grass growing on my chimney" (implying he was so committed to solitude that he hadn't cooked a meal for anyone).

"Big deal—you've driven away hospitality," countered the old man.

He wasn't impressed with their spiritual activity. In other words, not every spiritual activity or "God told me so" automatically earns God's stamp of approval.

How do we know the difference between "God told me so" and "I told myself so"? For the early holy fools, the key was found in one word: discernment. How do we know if our ideas are from God or the devil? Practice discernment, they said. How do I know if my urge to dance down the aisle and turn cartwheels during a worship service is holy folly or just a childish compulsion to get attention? Practice discernment. As athletes of God, not enough training can make us soft and flabby. But sometimes overtraining without proper rest and nutrition can kill even a healthy young athlete. How do we know where to draw the line? Practice discernment.

According to John Climacus, a seventh-century monk and spiritual guide, discernment is a "solid understanding of the will of God in all times, in all places, and in all things."[2] A more recent definition calls discernment "an inner light which enables [the follower of Christ] to advance steadily on the dark footpaths of life, distinguishing reliable landmarks from misleading ones, recognizing which thought comes from God, which is of human origin and which is demonic."[3] Without discernment we tend to sprain our ankles on the "dark footpath" of the spiritual journey. We push ourselves too hard or too soft. We read the signposts incorrectly. We miss the turns and then we plunge right over the cliff.

When I first read the actual writings of those ragged and wild desert fathers, I was shocked to find a consistent and sophisticated emphasis on discernment or, as they sometimes called it, discretion. "Some wear out their bodies with fasting," warned Antony, "but because they have no discretion, this only puts them further away from God."[4] "I tell you many have been stern with their bodies," counseled another hermit, "but have gained nothing by it because they did it without discretion."[5]

For all their radical rejection of compromised Christendom and their even more radical lifestyle in desert huts, their sense of discernment was informed by two very earthy qualities: God-given common sense and humane balance. "For goodness' sake," they sometimes lambasted their protégés, "have some common sense. Do you really think that demons are behind every spiritual struggle? Demons aren't always the problem; sometimes you're the problem. You're so stuck on yourself and doing what you want that it just feels like a demon."

One young man approached his mentor and whined, "Why does the enemy prevent me from doing good to my neighbor?"

"Oh, for crying out loud, you big baby [I'm paraphrasing here], why don't you leave the devil out of it and just say, 'I don't want to be kind to others'?"[6]

Second, as a whole (yes, there are notable exceptions), the stream of holy folly displays a striking sense of balance in the spiritual life. For instance, desert spirituality emphasized a balanced approach to practicing spiritual disciplines. Disciplines such as solitude, Scripture meditation, and prayer "should be at the proper time and in due measure" because "if they are used at the wrong time and to excess, they are useful for only a short time."[7] The desert fathers also recognized that not every spiritual "program" fits every human being. When it comes to the spiritual life, one size doesn't fit all. Beyond the clear boundaries of Christlikeness in love and holiness, solitude and hospitality, Scripture meditation and prayer, these holy fools were guided by a simple principle: "Each should do what is right for his own way of life." Balance is crucial in the discernment process.

One day a hunter wandered into the desert and watched in horror as Antony, the great man of God, relaxed and joked with a small group of monks. Apparently the hunter didn't appreciate Antony's lighthearted approach to the spiritual life. So Antony told him, "Put an arrow in your bow and then pull it back." The hunter complied and Antony said, "Okay, now pull it back further . . . and further . . . and further." Eventually the hunter complained, "Look, if I draw it back too far, the whole bow will snap in two." Antony responded, "It's the same way with God's work. If we always go to excess, straining and stretching ourselves in our spiritual life, we'll get tired and eventually we'll snap. Sometimes we need to kick back and relax."[8] (Antony, who founded his whole life on imitating Jesus, could have also mentioned the very Christlike activities of taking naps and attending dinner parties.)

The Great Experiment in Living like Jesus

How do I maintain balance? How do I know if I'm overtraining or undertraining? Developing the fine art of discernment never follows a set pattern for every would-be holy fool, but those practical, earthy, no-nonsense desert fathers did articulate guidelines for living a balanced spiritual life. They viewed life in the desert as a great experiment in living like Jesus. So like any scientific experiment, they tried things, they made mistakes, they threw out a hypothesis here and a theory there, they pursued new ideas, and then finally they drew conclusions and established guidelines. Sometimes they pushed things way too far (to be perfectly honest, sometimes they pushed things into the bizarre), so they'd lighten the load and try again. Over time they developed guidelines for walking in discernment on the spiritual journey in Christ. So although holy folly is often disturbing and provocative, the guidelines established by the holy fools are actually earthy and practical.

1. Master the Basics First

To begin the journey, the holy fools said, always master the basics before doing anything extraordinary. Actually, my college English professor said the same thing. As a college freshman and a budding young writer, I wanted my prose to shine. All the shiny prose writers I knew seemed to make exceptions to the basic rules of the English language. So I made exceptions too, but my English professor kept drawing red lines through my "shiny" prose. "It's not fair," I huffed. "How come Saul Bellow can make exceptions and I can't?" My professor calmly replied, "Because he's Saul Bellow and you're not. When you've mastered the basics of prose like Saul Bellow, I'll stop putting red lines on your paper."

Master the basics first and then worry about advanced techniques. According to my desert mentors, the same principle applies to the spiritual life. Learn the basics first. Master the Jesus tradition—the habits and practices he was known for here on earth—first and then worry about advanced flights into "deeper spirituality."

How did the holy fools master the basics of Jesus? To begin with, they immersed themselves in his life and teachings. Read the Gospel stories, they said. Memorize them. Meditate on them, allowing them to sink into every fiber of your being. Learn Jesus. Watch every move he made. Then immerse yourself in the story Jesus loved—the grand story of the Bible, the story of Israel, the Law, the Psalms, and the Prophets.

As a result, the Bible filled the day-to-day life of those ragged followers of Jesus. It was the air they breathed. When someone asked Antony, "What must I do to please God?" he replied, "Pay attention to what I advise you: wherever you go, always have God before your eyes; whatever you do, do it according to the testimony of Scripture." According to one historian, "The Scriptures were experienced as authoritative words which pierced the hearts of the monks. . . . *They appropriated Scripture so deeply that they came to be seen by their contemporaries as 'bearers of the Word.'*"[9] I've been called many things, but I can't remember the last time my contemporaries labeled me a "bearer of the Word."

2. Accept Beginner Status

As we immerse ourselves in Jesus, we make a startling discovery: We'll never *master* Jesus or his way to live. On the contrary, with great humility we realize that we'll never be a master at anything in the spiritual life. Actually, we discover that we'll remain a beginner for the rest of our lives.

In one story from the desert fathers, a young man renounced the world, trekked into the desert, holed himself in his cell, and brashly announced to everyone within earshot, "I am a solitary." When his neighboring hermits heard his announcement, they weren't impressed. They barged into his cell and threw him out. Then they forced him to make rounds to all the hermit cells in the area, humbly confessing, "Forgive me. I am not a solitary, I have only just begun to be a monk."[10] In the same way, Thomas Merton cautioned, "We do not want to be beginners. But let us be convinced of the fact that we will never be anything but beginners, all our life!"[11]

After nearly thirty years of following Jesus, after more than fifteen years of being in "professional ministry," it's humbling to say, "I'm still a beginner." Personally, I'd rather focus on my "growth" and "advancement" and "progress" in the spiritual life. I like little charts and diagrams and steps that prove, beyond the shadow of a doubt, I'm growing more like Jesus. Certainly, I have grown and I am making progress, but the longer I follow Jesus, the more I discover my need for fresh growth. Merton is right: I will never be anything but a beginner.

Personally, I don't find this demoralizing; I find it liberating. A little old nun helped me put it in a different light. Twelve years ago I attended a conference for young Christian writers at a small convent in Colorado, where we were learning the craft of writing and the process of getting published. Toward the end of our stay, an older nun approached my table and asked about the conference's "new writers" theme. "Oh, it's sort of a joke," I mocked. "I guess we're supposed to turn into writers by the end of this week." The nun (I think her name was Sister Gladys) raised a bony finger and, shaking it in my face, began to scold me. "Young man," she said, "never mock yourself for being a beginner. Every great endeavor has a small beginning. You may remain a beginner for a long time, but God loves beginners." Sister Gladys taught me to enjoy my perpetual beginner status—both as a writer and as a follower of Christ.

3. Reject "Mega-Spirituality"

Everyone wants to do great things for God—big missions, big plans, big programs, big feats of love and justice. Everyone (or so it seems) wants to join a mega-church and perform mega-deeds for God. Personally, I wouldn't mind becoming a mega-famous, mega-spiritual mega-pastor. At the very least I'd like to achieve "mega-ness" in one area of my life. In retrospect, the entire movement into the desert seems like a mega-heroic act of resistance, faithfulness, and witness. But the ragged desert holy fools consistently discouraged a preoccupation with mega-spirituality. Focus on mini-spirituality, they said. Practice small things. Focus on small acts of justice, compassion, faithfulness, and hospitality. Aim at obeying God and loving people in the context of the ordinary events in ordinary places.

You could raise the dead, argued one of the fathers, but

God would rather have you express your anger appropriately. You could embark on a pilgrimage and accomplish great things for God, but God would rather have you control your tongue.[12] When a young man asked for advice about a friend who kept floating up into the heavenly realms every time he started to pray, his wise old mentor said (I'm paraphrasing here), "For goodness' sake, the next time you see him floating toward heaven, grab his foot and yank him back to earth."[13] Sensational flights into religious experiences are worthless if you can't make it in this world as a human being. So keep your feet on the ground and focus on welcoming the next stranger who wanders into your neighborhood. Love—in the ordinary and concrete details of your life—is the hallmark of mini-spirituality.

In a very different context, the farmer-poet-essayist Wendell Berry observed, "It [he was referring to topsoil, but the "it" could just as appropriately apply to anything related to the Christian life] cannot be saved by heroic feats of gigantic technology but only by millions of small acts of restraints, conditioned by small fidelities, skills, and desires."[14] The small acts and small fidelities Berry describes really are the hardest to practice. I'd rather preach a great sermon to hundreds of people than practice reflective listening in a heated conversation with my wife. I'd rather write a popular book on contemplative prayer than actually pray for thirty minutes. I'd rather practice a spiritual discipline such as solitude, which aligns with my natural bent, than open my home to a stranger, which doesn't align with my natural bent.

A university student at our church recently sent me an e-mail about the beauty of mini-spirituality. As a single person in a church culture that tends to be couples-focused, she often feels lonely and excluded. After a women's Bible study centered around the problems faced by married women, she voiced her hurt and loneliness to one of the leaders. Rather than lecture her or give advice, this leader simply validated her hurt, hugged her, and then prayed with her. My university friend was deeply touched by this small, sacramental demonstration of love and concern. At the same time she lamented that these moments seem far too rare. I replied to her message by writing, "As the pastor of our church, I get to witness many of these small moments. They are beautiful, and we should never underestimate their importance. But you're right: These moments could sure happen more often." I guess the key is for us to be radically open to the Holy Spirit (see Romans 8:14) and then to be attentive to the presence of Jesus in the guise of whatever hurting, confused person happens to be in front of us at any given moment.

4. Respect Limits

Recently I saw a Christian book entitled something like *Know Your Limits—Then Ignore Them*. In all fairness, I never read the book, but the title seems to tap into a deep stream in our American psyche: the myth of limitless growth and potential. According to this mythology, you can do and be anything you want to. So if you want to be the president of the United States, go for it. If you want to become Miss America, the sky is the limit. If you want to join a pro football team, nothing should stop you—and if you're not big enough or fast enough, just take steroids. In the Christian realm, you can be a mother or father of three small children, work on your PhD, train for a marathon, work fifty hours a week, serve on a few committees in your church, have an hour-long prayer time, drive your children to eleven soccer, oboe, and stand-up comedy lessons . . . and never get tired. Just keep quoting verses like "I can do everything through Christ, who gives me strength" (Philippians 4:13) and you, too, can smash through your limits.

What a bunch of nonsense, said the desert fathers. We can't do everything. Know your limits and then respect them. According to one of the desert stories, a holy fool named John the Short announced to his community, "I want to live like the angels, living free from trouble and serving God unceasingly." So he stripped off his clothes and went buck naked into the desert.

Apparently John the Short found "angel life" a tad tougher than he'd imagined. Within a week he reappeared, knocking on the door of his mentor. "Who's there?" the brother asked.

"It's John. I'm back, so let me in."

"Oh, it couldn't be John," teased his mentor. "John became an angel, and he no longer lives among ordinary people like us."

"No, really; it's me, John."

The mentor ignored him and left him outside all night. In the morning, the mentor invited John in and said, "If you're a man, you will need to work in order to live. If you're really an angel, why do you want to come into my cell?" John asked for forgiveness and began to live like a man and not an angel.

None of us are angels or superheroes. Unlike the desert holy fools, I haven't been called by God to dwell in a hut, eat nothing but bread, and weave little mats. But every follower of Jesus in every age and within every calling has to heed the holy fools' advice and ask this question: Given the calling God has placed on my life, what does it mean to know and respect my limits?

I continually bump against specific fixed limits. God has called me to be a pastor on Long Island. I have a wife, four children, and three pets. All of them have particular needs and unique personalities—even the cats. I need about seven to eight hours of sleep a night. I'm forty-eight years old, not twenty-nine. My personal life falls apart if I consistently work more than sixty hours a week. Emotionally, I operate best when I have regular seasons to be alone. I can't mingle with people all week long. Does

God really want me to smash these limits? I used to think so, but now, like John the Short, I'm learning that I'm not an angel or a superhero. I'm a man who needs to live like an ordinary human being, respecting and even enjoying my God-ordained limits.

5. Find a Mentor and Companions

For the desert holy fools, the concept of embarking into the desert, fighting your demons, and living for Christ all by yourself was absolutely ludicrous. Everyone needs a mentor and companions, they advised. The desert path was littered with washed-out monks who had attempted the journey alone. Antony lamented, "I know of monks who fell after much toil and lapsed into madness because they trusted in their own works and did not give due heed to the commandment of him who says, 'Ask your father and he will tell you' (Deuteronomy 32:7, NIV)." Everyone needs a spiritual father or mother and a band of brothers and sisters.

Long before therapy and accountability groups, the desert fathers practiced a level of vulnerability that is simply astounding.

"How is it with you, my son?" asked one mentor.

The young man answered confidently, "Thanks to your prayers, I'm doing fine."

"Do any thoughts trouble you?" pressed the mentor.

Although the young man felt overwhelmed with temptation and evil thoughts, he replied, "No, today I'm doing quite well." He was too ashamed to reveal the truth.

The mentor sensed the trouble and confessed to his protégé, "Even after many years in the desert, and although everyone respects me as a wise old man, I'm still plagued by temptations and evil thoughts." Surprised by this honest confession, the young man opened his heart and confessed every thought to his mentor.[15]

On another occasion, a desert monk tried to understand a

certain passage of Scripture. He even fasted for seventy weeks, eating only one meal a week, but the passage still didn't make sense. Finally, he said, "I'm going to leave my cell and visit my brother. I'll ask him what this passage means."

As soon as he left his cell, an angel appeared to him and said, "The seventy weeks of fasting didn't bring you closer to God, but because you're humbling yourself and seeking out your brother, I will reveal the meaning of that Scripture passage to you."[16]

For the desert holy fools, everything—every thought, plan, spiritual practice, sin, or temptation—was laid bare before a mentor or a band of brothers or sisters in Christ. For years I rejected this earthy advice. I didn't think I needed a mentor or Christian community or accountability. Now I know I simply can't survive without these relationships. They're indispensable to my emotional and spiritual health.

Twice a month I meet with three brothers in Christ who ask me hard questions about my spiritual life, my ministry practices, and my secret sins and temptations. For our group it usually looks something like this: Each person spends about twenty minutes sharing from our lives—our joys, our struggles and challenges and temptations, our sins and failures. Since we've been meeting for more than four years now, we know the general themes of each of these areas. So we ask questions like, "Hey, Bill, last month you spoke about your bitterness toward someone in your church. How is that going? Have you been able to forgive him? Do you still feel angry? How can we pray for you today?"

6. Experience Joy

We all know "church people" who, although they display dedication, discipline, and commitment, also emit a toxic level of cranky and judgmental spirituality. So they serve and give and pray, but they also whine and gripe and moan about nearly everything. They're never really happy about Jesus or the church or just about anything. They have made it their mission to be crabby Christians for God.

But should spiritual dedication lead to spiritual grumpiness? Jesus doesn't seem to think so. To the contrary, Jesus views joy as a quality of God. Three times in Luke 15, Jesus referred to the joy of his Father over one sinner who repents. God experiences joy. Do I? The desert fathers weren't exactly spiritual comedians, but they did practice radical hospitality, opening their cells and sharing their goods, without crankiness or crabbiness. They actually liked people.

Walking with discernment involves taking an honest assessment of my life. Is there joy in my life? Do I find genuine joy in serving God and loving others? Am I regularly rejoicing over the reality of lost prodigals making their way back home? Or am I more like the older brother—responsible and dedicated but stiff, grim, and utterly unhappy? Does my approach to the spiritual life make me more joyful, or does it just make me crabby? I need to make a conscious effort to evaluate my life and determine where I am healthy and unhealthy, balanced and unbalanced.

QUESTIONS FOR REFLECTION

Thomas Merton said, "Many of our most cherished plans for the glory of God are only inordinate passion in disguise." Can you think of a time when you thought you had cherished plans for God but they were really more about your own passion?

What would discernment look like in different areas of your life? What are some steps you can take to start developing discernment?

Am I mastering the basics of Jesus? Am I constantly immersing myself in the story of Jesus and the grand story that Jesus loved?

Am I humble enough to admit my beginner status? I'm not an advanced student and I never will be. Am I content with that?

Are the small areas of obedience and faithfulness more important to me than the big areas? Am I hankering after mega-spirituality, or am I content with mini-spirituality?

What are the specific ways in which my life is limited? How could I show more respect for the limits God has placed on my life?

Do I have honest, accountable relationships with a mentor or brothers and sisters in Christ? Am I honest about my sins, temptations, and struggles? Do these people know me well enough to tell me when my life is unbalanced?

Is there joy in my life, or does my approach to the spiritual life just make me crabby?

Creating a Movement of Holy Folly

THIRTY YEARS AGO, during my senior year in high school, a handful of friends gathered to pray about our last year before we scattered to college and other places. In the midst of our calm prayer meeting, somebody had the chutzpah to ask God to miraculously change the hearts of everyone in our entire senior class—all 477 students. In a major adrenaline rush, we all exclaimed, "What a great idea! We'll just tell God to bring everyone to personal faith in Christ in less than a year!" So before the fall quarter we sent a very nice personal letter to every one of our fellow seniors. It said something like, "Hi, we're followers of Jesus and we love you. We're praying that you will have the best year of your life and that you'll come to know Jesus before June. And if you ever want to talk or pray about anything, we're here for you." And then we started earnestly beseeching God to save 477 people by June.

It didn't happen. We didn't even come close to our goal—although everyone agreed it was a sensitive and well-crafted letter. For twenty-five years I felt sheepish about our silly adrenaline-laced prayer, and I quietly vowed to avoid such outlandish ideas. The entire plan was just a wee bit presumptuous. I mean, where did we get the idea that God had promised to save 477 people on our timetable—and through our witness, no less? How arrogant and absurd!

But now that I'm in my late forties, I'm not worried about acting outlandish or foolish. I'm just worried that I'll act "wise" and "moderate"—and utterly safe and bland and cold. I'm worried that in the name of decency and order I'll never do anything foolish. Lately, I keep thinking about that wild group of fiery high school seniors gathering in the basement of a suburban home, excitedly discussing our plans to take over the world—or at least our local high school—with a revolution of love and new creation. We never asked, "What will others think?" or "This has never been tried before," or "This is too dangerous and impractical."

Perhaps it's time for another revolution of holy folly. For the past ten years, I've been walking with holy fools. At first they felt like unwelcome and untidy guests on my journey. I was embarrassed to be associated with them. Now I can't imagine journeying through life without them. Yes, at times they look bizarre, but like an eccentric uncle at your family gatherings, they eventually grow on you in their quirkiness. So I can say without reservation that I like these holy fools. I may not always agree with their strategies or tactics. I may not imitate every detail of their crazy antics, but I like their chutzpah, their gutsy, daring, wild, messy, at times in-your-face and at times entirely winsome approach to the spiritual life.

A friend recently asked what I hoped to accomplish for the Kingdom of God by writing this book. In answer to my friend's question, I hope that two things will happen. First, I want to be a different person because of my association with this motley collection of dead and alive people called the holy fools. I want God to change my heart and make me more like Jesus, the ultimate holy fool. God is already doing that. The holy fools are now under my skin and even in my dreams. People like Saint Francis, Hudson Taylor, Antony, and my friends Leon and Nancy and Willis (among many others) are here to stay.

Second, I want God to raise up a new band of holy fools who love Jesus with reckless abandon, exhibiting all the characteristics of holy folly. I want a new generation of believers to say, "I want to be a holy fool."

So before we dismiss the holy fools as wild-eyed lunatics, perhaps it's time to consider some basic questions posed by their stories.

> When was the last time I poured out love for God with reckless abandon?
>
> When was the last time I spent a day or an hour in my hermitage, quietly listening to God?
>
> When was the last time I left my safe Christian ghetto and engaged and pursued ragged sinners?
>
> When was the last time I actually felt like an athlete in my pursuit of spiritual growth?
>
> When was the last time nobody noticed or people even criticized me when I served God, but I didn't even care?

When was the last time I engaged my brokenness, offered it
to God, and felt his power surging through the weak and broken places of my life?

When was the last time I was called "foolish" or even
"unpractical" just because I love Jesus?

So once again, I have this strange longing to journey up the
stream of holy folly. Once again, I'm uttering this strange and
dangerous prayer: "Father God, I want to be a holy fool, loving
Jesus with reckless abandon, drinking deeply from the stream of
holy folly. Come Holy Spirit, awaken me! Awaken me to a life of
compassion, vulnerability, discipline, and spiritual passion."

This adventure of holy folly is not one to embark on alone.
But as we look ahead of us on this journey, we see that we're trac-
ing the footsteps of a band of reckless, ragged-edged, and wildly
alive followers of God.

Will you dare to join them?

Recommended Reading

Bondi, Roberta. *To Love as God Loves*. Philadelphia: Fortress Press, 1987. A fine introduction to desert spirituality.

Chan, Simon. *Spiritual Theology*. Downers Grove, IL: InterVarsity Press, 1998. A fresh look at spiritual disciplines, including some excellent material on developing a "rule of life."

Chryssavgis, John. *In the Heart of the Desert*. Bloomington, IN: World Wisdom, Inc., 2003. An excellent summary of the desert fathers from a Greek Orthodox perspective.

Cowart, John. *People Whose Faith Got Them into Trouble*. Downers Grove, IL: InterVarsity Press, 1990. Great stories about historical holy fools such as Saint Patrick, Mary Slessor, and Hudson Taylor.

Foster, Richard J. *Celebration of Discipline*. San Francisco: Harper and Row Publishers, 1978. The classic work on spiritual disciplines.

Green, Joel B., and **Mark D. Baker.** *Recovering the Scandal of the Cross*. Downers Grove, IL: InterVarsity Press, 2000. A good resource that explains the New Testament's teaching on the folly of the Cross.

Hengel, Martin. *Crucifixion*. Philadelphia: Fortress Press, 1977. A superb, scholarly overview of crucifixions in the ancient world.

Kierkegaard, Søren. *Provocations*. Compiled and edited by Charles E. Moore. Farmington, PA: The Plough Publishing House, 2002. Kierkegaard challenges us to reject mediocre faith and live passionately for Christ. Contains parables, essays, quotes, and prayers.

Lane, Belden. *The Solace of Fierce Landscapes*. New York: Oxford University Press, 1998. A theological treatise on desert spirituality.

Merton, Thomas. *Contemplative Prayer.* New York: Image Books, 1969. A slim though profound volume on the nature of contemplative prayer and the presence of Christ.

_____. *Thoughts in Solitude.* New York: Farrar, Straus and Giroux, 1958. This book is still relevant to our need for solitude in a hectic culture.

_____. *The Wisdom of the Desert.* New York: New Directions Books, 1970. Contains quotes and stories from the desert fathers. The introduction explains the motivation and beauty of the desert movement.

Nomura, Yushi. *Desert Wisdom.* Maryknoll, NY: Orbis Books, 1982. A collection of quotes and stories from the desert fathers, including moving drawings and a fine introduction by Henri Nouwen.

Nouwen, Henri. *The Way of the Heart.* New York: Ballantine Books, 1983. As always, Nouwen is gentle, challenging, and practical all at once. This is a wonderful overview of desert spirituality.

Rolheiser, Ronald. *The Shattered Lantern.* New York: Crossroad Publishing Company, 2001. One of the best books on contemplative prayer I've read. Rolheiser helps us understand contemplation and how culture prevents us from experiencing God's presence.

Vanier, Jean. *From Brokenness to Community.* New York: Paulist Press, 1992. A beautiful little book consisting of two lectures delivered at Harvard. A profound meditation on God's power in our weakness.

Waddell, Helen, trans. *The Desert Fathers.* New York: Vintage Books, 1998. One of the classic collections of stories and quotes from the desert fathers. Includes a fine introduction from Basil Pennington.

Ward, Benedicta. *The Desert Fathers.* New York: Penguin Books, 2003. A classic collection of sayings from the desert fathers; arranged by topic.

Willard, Dallas. *The Spirit of the Disciplines.* San Francisco: Harper and Row Publishers, 1988. This book offers a vision for the *spirit* of the disciplines—not just what they are, but how they work in our lives.

Notes

Holy Fools: The Ants in Our Spiritual Pants

1. The desert fathers and mothers were a loosely organized group of Christ followers that arose in the fourth century after Christ. They were inspired by a man named Antony, the first desert father, who left his comfortable home and settled deep in the wildness of the desert. Although he spent much of his time in prayer and Scripture reading, Antony also had a vibrant ministry of compassion, healing, mentoring, and teaching that touched the lives of thousands around him. Within forty years of Antony's death (around 356), the movement of desert spirituality began to blossom as men and women abandoned a compromised church culture in order to seek God and build community in the wilderness. Some of them lived alone; others joined into small bands of community with organized structure and leadership. Some pushed their spiritual practices into a morbid direction, while many maintained a balanced but challenging approach to spiritual disciplines.

2. John Polkinghorne, *Quarks, Chaos and Christianity* (New York: Crossroad, 2000), 10.

Chapter 1: Discovering God's Ragged Children

1. The great Jewish theologian A. J. Heschel once commented on the prophets: His images must not shine, they must burn. . . . His words are often slashing, even horrid—designed to shock rather than to edify. *The Prophets* (New York: Harper and Row, 1962), 8.

2. If you want to find out more about the early desert Christians, I've included at the end of this book a list of sources that have been helpful to me in learning about their adventures in holy folly—and embarking on my own.

3. I am indebted to Wendy Wright for this original idea—although I did see the same billboard when I was growing up in Minnesota.

4. This comment was made by a pagan philosopher named Porphyry in his ancient work *Against the Christians*. It is quoted in Thomas Molnar, *The Pagan Temptation* (Grand Rapids, MI: Eerdmans, 1987), 27.

5. The classic study on this topic was written by a German scholar named Martin Hengel in his book *Crucifixion* (Philadelphia: Fortress Press, 1977). He describes crucifixion as a "barbaric form of execution of utmost cruelty"—the supreme Roman penalty that was reserved for "rebellious foreigners, violent criminals, and robbers." Hengel helps us put crucifixion in its proper historical context: "The cross was not just a matter of indifference, just any kind of death. It was an utterly offensive affair, 'obscene' in the original sense of the word" (page 22).

6. We don't know for sure the nature of what happened here. We do know that this kind of contact between a man—especially a Jewish man who was also a rabbi—and a woman was highly inappropriate, crossing boundaries of sexual propriety. And yet Jesus allowed it. The text does not say why he allowed something so blatantly inappropriate to happen, but I have a hunch that Jesus knew she was loving him the only way that she knew how to love him.

Chapter 2: Subverting Self-Righteousness

1. I guess Clive paved the way for me on this one! Following C. S. Lewis, I'm using *damn* in its theological rather than its frivolous sense. Our seriousness can wrap us so tightly in a web of self-righteousness that the spiritual life literally gets sucked out of us. We become mere husks, perhaps even spiritually damned husks, of spiritual men and women.

2. Helmut Thielicke, *The Waiting Father* (New York: Harper and Row, 1959), 33–34.

3. To find out more about Romuald, see John Saward, *Perfect Fools* (New York: Oxford University Press, 1980), 49–51.

4. Quoted in Thomas C. Peters, *The Christian Imagination* (San Francisco: Ignatius Press, 2000), 124.

5. Adapted from Leonard Sweet, *SoulTsunami* (Grand Rapids: Zondervan, 1999), 61.

6. *New York Times Magazine* (September 10, 2006), 58.

7. Lance Morrow, *Evil: An Investigation* (New York: Basic Books, 2003), 25.

8. Wendy Wright, "Fools for Christ," *Weavings*, IX:6 (November/December 1994): 29.

9. Quoted in Conrad Hyers, *The Comic Vision and the Christian Faith* (Cleveland: Pilgrim Press, 1981), 20–21.

Chapter 3: Demolishing Ghetto Walls

1. Iulia de Beausobre, *Creative Suffering* (Oxford: SLG Press, 1984), 32–34.

2. Kallistos Ware, *The Inner Kingdom* (Crestwood, NY: St. Vladimir's Seminary Press, 2000), 175.

3. Philip Yancey, *The Jesus I Never Knew* (Grand Rapids, MI: Zondervan, 1995), 149.

4. Craig Keener, *Commentary on Matthew* (Grand Rapids, MI: William B. Eerdmans, 1999), 297.

5. Adapted from Belden Lane, *The Solace of Fierce Landscapes* (New York: Oxford University Press, 1998), 176.

6. Denis Haack, "What Does Winsome Look Like?: Part 2," *Critique*, no. 9 (2001): 10.

7. Interestingly, the Greek word is in the present imperative, meaning "do not habitually call" or "don't make a practice of calling."

8. This ultrastrict Jewish community was called the Essenes. The Essenes lived in Qumran, a desert site, from about 130 BC to AD 70. "Well-to-do persons in the Greco-Roman world usually invited people of somewhat lower social status in return for receiving honor, but these invitees would still be relatively respectable, not absolute dependents or beggars, as crippled, lame and blind people would be in that society. . . . The crippled, lame and blind were not permitted on the premises of the probably Essene community at Qumran." Craig S. Keener, *The IVP Bible Background Commentary New Testament* (Downers Grove, IL: InterVarsity Press, 1993), 229–30.

9. The life of Abba Antony is a prime example of this commitment to hospitality. "Antony does not fit our standard picture of the hermit. Very quickly in his career he found himself visited by potential disciples. Even more, Antony was a public figure; he did not remain in the desert with these disciples. At one point in his career he journeyed into the great city of Alexandria where he publicly encouraged the martyrs who were being tried and killed. Later in his long life, back in the desert, he was visited by soldiers, government officials, pagan priests and philosophers, local landowners and peasants. All of these came to him for advice on the affairs of the secular world as well as of the spiritual." Roberta C. Bondi, *To Love as God Loves* (Philadelphia: Fortress Press, 1987), 15.

Chapter 4: Receiving the Gift of Tears

1. Jean Leclercq, *The Love of Learning and the Desire for God* (New York: Fordham University Press, 1974), 37–38.

2. John Climacus, *The Ladder of Divine Ascent* (Mahwah, NJ: Paulist Press, 1982), 139.

3. Francis (or Francesco Bernardone) was born in 1182, the son of a wealthy, tyrannical cloth merchant. For the first half of his life there was nothing particularly remarkable about Francesco. "A spoiled rich man's son, he became in his teens a dissolute layabout, whose supremely practical father tried repeatedly and unsuccessfully to interest him in the particulars of the cloth trade." After participating in a local civil war, which left him languishing with malaria in a dank prison cell for over a year, the spoiled Francis started to ponder his spiritual life. On a bright summer afternoon in 1205, Francis returned from an errand with his father and took refuge in the shade of the San Damiano chapel in Assisi. There he heard Jesus speak to him, commissioning Francis to follow him and rebuild the church. That was the turning point in Francis's life. "An irreligious man, he had found the love of his life—God, or more precisely, God revealed in Jesus—and this discovery made sense of everything else, putting all others, whether people or things, in their proper perspective." For more information about Francis, see Thomas Cahill, *Mysteries of the Middle Ages* (New York: Doubleday, 2006), 159–60.

4. This is how Julien Green describes Francis's encounter: "Inside the cave the hours were passing, not in bliss, as before, but in the agony of repentance. Very few men have wept as Francis did. In a flood of tears, he reviewed his past, which filled him with horror, and for the first time he became aware of the enormity of his sin." *God's Fool* (San Francisco: Harper and Row Publishers, 1983), 69.

5. Kathleen Norris, *Amazing Grace: A Vocabulary of Faith* (New York: Riverhead Books, 1998), 2.

6. Garrison Keillor, *We Are Still Married* (New York: Penguin Books, 1990), 22.

7. Irma Zaleski, *The Way of Repentance* (New York: Continuum, 1999), 11–12.

8. Quoted in James Houston, *Joyful Exiles* (Downers Grove, IL: InterVarsity Press, 2006), 25–26.

9. Flannery O'Connor, *The Complete Works of Flannery O'Connor* (New York: The Noon Day Press, 1990), 333.

10. I include voices like Ehrenreich not because I agree with her (actually, I strongly disagree with her) but because I want to know what those outside "our camp" think about us and our faith. We need to hear their critique, right or wrong; there is something we can learn from these "outsiders" and even from opponents to our faith. Ehrenreich definitely has an inaccurate view of John Bunyan's life, but I do find her perception of him—and us—interesting. Barbara Ehrenreich, *Dancing in the Streets* (New York: Metropolitan Books, 2006), 144.

11. This is taken from John Chrysostom's sermon "Dead to Sin."

12. Dietrich Bonhoeffer, *Life Together* (New York: Harper and Row, 1976), 114.

13. Green, *God's Fool*, 69–70.

Chapter 5: Engaging Our Brokenness

1. Christopher de Vinck, *The Power of the Powerless* (New York: Doubleday, 1988), 9.

2. Ibid., 31.

3. Marva J. Dawn, *Powers, Weakness, and the Tabernacling of God* (Grand Rapids, MI: William B. Eerdmans, 2001), 36–37.

4. Quoted in Thomas V. Morris, *Making Sense of It All* (Grand Rapids, MI: William B. Eerdmans, 1992), 31–45.

5. Thomas Merton, *Thoughts in Solitude* (New York: Farrar, Straus and Giroux, 1958), 3.

6. Ibid., 25–26.

7. Unfortunately, this painting is part of a private collection and is not available for reprinting. However, you might be able to find it at your local library or online at http://www.galeriedada.com/onthewall. php?id=00001794. There is also an extensive collection of Rouault at Saint Procopius Abbey in Lisle, Illinois, http://www.procopius.org.

8. Jean Vanier, *From Brokenness to Community* (New York: Paulist Press, 1992), 19–21.

9. Lewis portrays this idea in *The Problem of Pain* (New York: Macmillan Publishing Co., 1962), 101.

Chapter 6: Training as an Athlete of God

1. Quoted in Robert Ellsberg, *The Saints' Guide to Happiness* (New York: North Point Press, 2003), 12.

2. This is a well-known story, but it can be found in *Desert Wisdom*, translation and art by Yushi Nomura (Maryknoll, NY: Orbis Books, 1982), 99. If you want a very good and artistic depiction of the desert fathers and mothers, this is a great book with a fine introduction by Henri Nouwen.

3. C. S. Lewis, *Mere Christianity* (New York: Macmillan Publishing Company, 1977), 65.

4. Nomura, *Desert Wisdom,* 17.

5. Simon Chan, *Spiritual Theology* (Downers Grove, IL: InterVarsity Press, 1998), 191–92.

6. Saint Benedict's world was marked by trouble and uncertainty, both politically and religiously. "The fall of Rome in A.D. 410, seventy years before the birth of St. Benedict, had been a traumatic shock to the entire

civilized world, and since then the invasions of successive barbarian hordes had begun to dismember the empire. . . . The church too was torn apart . . . split theologically, particularly on the question of grace, which was a major concern in the fifth century. Christians must have looked back with nostalgia to the age of the Fathers and asked themselves if ever again the church could produce a St. Augustine and a City of God to hold out the promise of peace and order and light on a scene which seemed instead to be rapidly descending into chaos." Esther de Waal, *Seeking God* (Collegeville, MN: Liturgical Press, 2001), 13.

7. Saint Benedict, *The Rule of Saint Benedict* (Westminster, MD: The Newman Press, 1952), 13.

8. To find out more about the classic spiritual disciplines, see Richard J. Foster's book *Celebration of Discipline* (New York: Harper and Row, 1978).

9. For information on locating a retreat center, see Timothy Jones's book *A Place for God: A Guide to Spiritual Retreats and Retreat Centers* (New York: Image Books, 2000).

10. In a sermon dated July 16, 2006, I gave a whimsical list of "ten really good things to do on the Sabbath": (1) Prepare for and enjoy worship by saying, "This is the day that the Lord has made! Let us rejoice and be glad in it!"; (2) Take a nap and don't set the alarm; (3) Make something creative—supper, soup, a poem, a song, a floral arrangement, a bookshelf (unless you're already a professional carpenter); (4) Invite people over for dinner; (5) Enjoy creation—do not go to the mall or shop online; (6) Delight as God delights in his good work; (7) Take a walk; (8) Write a letter or make a phone call to a friend, family member, or even an "enemy," but do not check your work e-mail; (9) Find something that makes you laugh; (10) Go to a soccer game, but don't yell at the officials or your kids; just talk to your neighbors.

11. I generally read one psalm a day—although there is no specific "rule" about this. If something in the psalm hits a deep chord within me, I usually stop and ponder it and maybe stop for the day. The important thing is to go through the psalms in order so I don't skip any that I find irrelevant or scary or too emotional or whatever. It usually takes me almost a year to go through all 150 psalms.

12. It's true that the desert fathers and mothers were separated from the

world to some degree in their solitary cells. But they were not haters of their fellow humans. "Story after story, saying after saying bespeaks . . . an immensely loving and truly touching care not only for the new-comers who came into their midst and for the venerable ancients among them but for any troubled one. Edifying, to say the least, was their response to visitors, whether they were humble seekers, true pil-grims, or just the curious and those who wanted to go home and tell their story. One cannot help but be touched by the ready way in which these desert dwellers set aside their own much-loved practices and their precious solitude to welcome these visitors and make them as com-fortable as their limited means and inhospitable setting allowed." Helen Waddell, *The Desert Fathers* (New York: Vintage Books, 1998), xviii.

13. Athanasius, *The Life of Antony and the Letters of Marcellinus* (New York: Paulist Press, 1980), 42.

14. Quoted in Ellsberg, *The Saints' Guide to Happiness*, 3.

15. Kathleen Norris, *Dakota: A Spiritual Geography* (New York: Ticknor and Fields, 1993), 23.

Chapter 7: Praying Like a Hermit

1. Thomas Merton, *The Inner Experience* (New York: HarperOne, 2004), 111. In another book, Merton writes disparagingly of the "cult of sitting still," the illusion that stillness "in itself has a magic power to solve all problems and bring man into contact with God." He labels this an "evasion," a "lack of honesty," a "trifling with grace and a flight from God." Thomas Merton, *Contemplative Prayer* (Garden City, NY: Image Books, 1971), 89.

2. Quoted in Os Guinness, *The Call* (Nashville: W Publishing Group, 1998), 10.

3. Ronald Rolheiser, *The Shattered Lantern* (New York: Crossroad, 2004), 201.

4. Ronald Rolheiser explores this much better than I do. Please read his book entitled *The Shattered Lantern*.

5. Thomas Merton, *Thoughts in Solitude*, 79.

6. Roman Guardini defines internal noise as "the inner turmoil, the whirl of thoughts, the drive of desire, the restlessness and worries of the mind, the burden of care, the wall of dullness—or whatever that may be which

fills our interior world as the rubble fills an abandoned well." *The Virtues* (Chicago: Regnery, 1963), 147.

7. I want to emphasize that study certainly has its place alongside meditation. It is one of the classic spiritual disciplines that opens us to God's grace (see chapter 6). Thomas Merton describes the two disciplines this way: "Meditation and study can, of course, be closely related. In fact, study is not spiritually fruitful unless it leads to some kind of meditation. By study we seek the truth in books or in some other source outside our own minds. In meditation we strive to absorb what we have already taken in. . . . In study we can be content with an idea or a concept that is true. We can be content to know about truth. Meditation is for those who are not satisfied with a merely objective knowledge about life, about God—about ultimate realities. They want to experience the deepest realities of life by living them. Meditation is the means to that end." Thomas Merton, *Spiritual Direction and Meditation* (Collegeville, MN: The Order of St. Benedict, 1960), 53. My goal in this chapter is to focus on the process of meditation since most of us have never learned how to "savor" a portion of Scripture.

8. Thomas Merton, *Contemplative Prayer*, 29.

9. Adapted from *Flame in the Snow* (Springfield, IL: Templegate Publishers, 1997), Julia de Beausobre's fine biography about Saint Seraphim of Sarov.

Chapter 8: Practicing Secret Goodness

1. Admittedly, this is one of the strangest aspects of holy folly. The desert fathers weren't advocating a life of hypocrisy, dishonesty, or low self-esteem (as in, "Aw, shucks, we all know I'm a saint, but I'm going to act like a creep so you think badly of me"). The point behind the holy fool's practice of secret goodness is to avoid our constant drive to turn holy men and women into celebrities, to honor the saint rather than the Redeemer who makes sinners into saints. Did the holy fools take it too far? Of course they did. Should we imitate every detail of their excesses? Absolutely not. But while we can clearly see their excesses, we're largely blind to our excessive and ridiculous quasi worship of Christian "celebrities." Thus, we must have Ms. Famous Preacher and Mr. Amazing Worship Leader

video-fed onto the big screen during our worship services because only they can move us into the presence of God.

2. See Saward, *Perfect Fools*, 25.

3. Ware, *The Inner Kingdom*, 160–80.

4. Saward, *Perfect Fools*, 19.

5. Both of these stories are from Belden Lane, *The Solace of Fierce Landscapes* (New York: Oxford University Press, 1998), 170.

6. Dallas Willard, *The Divine Conspiracy* (New York: HarperCollins, 1998), 283.

7. Marc Foley, O.C.D., *The Love That Keeps Us Sane* (Mahwah, NJ: Paulist Press, 2000), 25.

8. David Elkind, *All Grown Up and No Place to Go* (Reading, MA: Addison Wesley Publishing Company, 1984), 33.

9. This phrase is from a book by Christopher Lasch called *The Culture of Narcissism: American Life in an Age of Diminishing Expectations* (New York: W. W. Norton and Co., 1979).

10. Willard, *The Divine Conspiracy*, 191.

11. Lewis, *Mere Christianity*, 112.

12. Saint Francis de Sales, *Introduction to the Devout Life* (Garden City, NY: Image Books, 1972), 215.

Chapter 9: Living in Joyful Surrender

1. Lewis, *Mere Christianity*, 190.

2. Francis was doing this not to be sensational but as a way of severing ties with the wealth and family that constituted his former life. It was a youthful and perhaps excessive way to physically demonstrate that he had severed his addiction to a life of privilege, wealth, and coldness toward others. Like baptism, it was a decisive, radical, bodily, and public way to break with the old life and enter a new life with Christ. Was it immature? Perhaps. But Francis never did anything halfheartedly.

3. Søren Kierkegaard, *Provocations* (Farmington, PA: The Plough Publishing House, 2002), 16–17.

4. Anne Lamott, *Bird by Bird* (New York: Anchor Books, 1994), 21–22.

5. Waddell, *The Desert Fathers*, xvi.

6. Quoted in Kathleen Norris, *The Quotidian Mysteries* (New York: Paulist Press, 1998), 70–71.

Chapter 10: Walking with Discernment

1. Merton, *Thoughts in Solitude*, 115.

2. Quoted in Stelios Ramfos, *Like a Pelican in the Wilderness* (Brookline, MA: Holy Cross Orthodox Press, 2000), 223.

3. Ibid.

4. Benedicta Ward, *The Desert Fathers* (London: Penguin Books, 2003), 88.

5. Ibid., 111.

6. Ibid., 103–104.

7. Ibid., 93.

8. Ibid., 88.

9. Douglas Burton-Christie, *The Word in the Desert* (New York: Oxford University Press, 1993), 4.

10. Ward, *The Desert Fathers*, 116.

11. Merton, *Contemplative Prayer*, 37.

12. Ward, *The Desert Fathers*, 91, 96.

13. Ibid., 116.

14. Wendell Berry, *Sex, Economy, Freedom and Community* (New York: Pantheon Books, 1992), 13–14.

15. Waddell, *The Desert Fathers*, 144.

16. Ibid., 125.